MONUMENT

at Warren, Pa., to General Joseph Warren for whom the town
and county were named. Erected 1910 by the Tidioute Chapter,
Daughters of the American Revolution. It bears a tablet ''In
Honor of the Soldiers and Sailors of the Revolutionary War Who
Are Buried in Warren County.''

REVOLUTIONARY SOLDIERS OF WARREN COUNTY, PENNSYLVANIA

BY

LUCY M. DAVIS COWAN

Southern Historical Press, Inc.
Greenville, South Carolina

Originally Published 1926:
New York, NY.

SOUTHERN HISTORICAL PRESS, INC.
PO BOX 1267
Greenville, SC   29601

ISBN #978-1-63914-109-8

Printed in the United States of America

LUCY MARIE DAVIS COWAN

Mrs. Lucy Marie Davis Cowan died on Nov. 20, 1925, at Warren, Pa., as a result of an accident in which she was severely burned. A few weeks previous, she completed the manuscript of the present work which was in press at the time of her death.

Mrs. Cowan was born in Watkins, N. Y., and was the daughter of Lot B. and Julia (Hudson) Davis. On Sept. 24, 1878, she married Willis Cowan, son. of Ephraim and Malvina (King) Cowan, of Warren, Pa. After her marriage, she resided in Warren until the death of Mr. Cowan, July 14, 1923. Later she made her home in Washington, D. C. Among her ancestors were the Mayflower Pilgrims: John Alden, Richard Warren and William Brewster, also the following Revolutionary Soldiers: John Bartlett, Benjamin Dow, Alpheus Davis and Asa Hudson.

She was one of the earliest members in Warren County, of the National Society of the Daughters of the American Revolution. She was a member of the Tidioute Chapter and a charter member of the Gen. Joseph. Warren Chapter, which was later organized in Warren, Pa. As the second Regent, and for many years as Registrar, she accomplished much in furthering the interest of the D. A. R. She was a member of Trinity Memorial Episcopal Church and Trinity Guild of Warren, Pa., and of a number of patriotic, historical and social organizations.[1]

Mrs. Cowan was considered an authority on the genealogy of Warren County families and on the military records of Warren County men. She left an unfinished manuscript entitled ''Warren County Soldiers in the War of 1812.''

---

[1] Member of the Warren County Historical Society; Charter Member of the Woman's Club, Warren, Pa.; Charter Member and Organizing Secretary of the Warren County Chapter of the American Red Cross; Member of the Society of the Descendants of Robert and Mary Warren Bartlett; Member of the National Genealogical Society, Washington, D. C.; Charter Member of the Gen. Wm. Irvine Chapter Daughters 1812–14, Warren, Pa.

FOREWORD

In 1908–9, the late Mrs. Charlotte Sink Cummings, then Regent of the Tidioute Chapter, National Society of Daughters of the American Revolution, reached the conclusion that the Chapter was strong enough to undertake the work of collecting the names and records of services of the men buried in Warren County, Pennsylvania, who had served in the American Revolution, and erecting in the county seat a memorial inscribed with their names. She asked me to assist her and we worked literally night and day at a task that proved a difficult undertaking. Finally, on July 4, 1910, the Tidioute Chapter dedicated the beautiful monument in Warren, in the triangular park at the intersection of Pennsylvania and Third Avenues.

The chief speaker on that occasion was the late Hon. Charles Warren Stone, President of the Warren County Historical Society. At that time he obtained from me a promise to collect personal records of the Revolutionary Soldiers of Warren County and place them in permanent form. This small volume is the fulfillment of my promise to Mr. Stone.

The gathering of these records has been difficult, involving research carried on through a period of years. It will be found that several names have been added to the original list of soldiers inscribed on the monument. Although the accounts are far from complete, it has been decided to issue the book, trusting that its contents may be interesting to not a few.

I wish to acknowledge with sincere thanks the assistance given me by the Commissioners of Warren County. My thanks are also due to Mr. Byron Barnes Horton of Sheffield and to Mr. Gurney A. Jewell of North Warren, for assistance in research.

MRS. LUCY M. DAVIS COWAN.

October, 1925

CONTENTS

REVOLUTIONARY SOLDIERS OF WARREN COUNTY, PENNSYLVANIA

MILITARY SERVICES OF SOLDIERS WHOSE RECORDS HAVE BEEN PROVED

RICHARD ARTERS, 1758–1843

He was born in Pennsylvania in 1758, died in 1843, and was buried in the old cemetery at Tidioute, Pa. His wife, who was Mary Ann Bowman, is buried beside him. Their stones are still standing but are so badly weathered that only the names are discernible.

His name appears in the seventh class in Capt. Robert Mean's Company, Eighth Battalion, Cumberland County Militia, commanded by Col. Alex. Brown, for the years 1780, 1781, 1782. (Pa. Archives, 5th Series, vol. 6, p. 566.)

Richard Arters was of English parentage. He and his son Thomas removed from Lewistown, Mifflin County, Pa., to Warren County and settled in 1806 on the Allegheny River at the mouth of Tidioute Creek, on a tract of 400 acres surveyed by John Spangler. This was the first permanent settlement in that part of the county. Richard Arters soon after removed to a tract on the southeast side of the Allegheny, nearly opposite the lower part of Tidioute Borough, where he cleared a small farm. He was probably the first permanent settler in what is now Limestone Township. He had a large family, among whom was Thomas, born 1787, who built the first framed house in Deerfield Township in 1824. (Warren Co. History, pp. 457, 493.)

He was taxed in Brokenstraw Township 1815 to 1818 inclusive, **and** again in 1821; in Deerfield Township, 1822 to 1824 inclusive.

In the Census of 1820 he is listed as a resident of Conewango Township.

The name has been spelled Arthers, Arthurs and Arters. The latter form is used by Richard's descendants.

JAMES ARTHUR

He died at Youngsville, Pa., date unknown.

His name appears on the roll of Capt. Samuel Watson's Company, from Jan. 5, 1776 to Nov. 25, 1776. He enlisted Feb. 2, 1776, in the 2d Pa. Battalion, Col. Arthur St. Clair. (Pa. Archives, 5th Series, vol. 2, p. 112.)

He came to Warren County in 1798 with his father, Robert Arthur, Sen. In 1808, he was taxed in Warren; in 1816, he was assessed in Brokenstraw Township and in Conewango Township where he owned a saw mill. In 1824, he was a deputy sheriff. He was recorded as a lumberman in the first assessment of Warren Borough in 1833. (Warren Co. History, pp. 133, 139, 140, 148, 338, vi.)

He was named on the Tax Lists as follows: Conewango Township, 1806 to 1832, inclusive, excepting the years 1807, 1810 and 1817; Brokenstraw Township, 1814 and 1816; Warren Borough, 1833 to 1835, inclusive.

LIEUT. ROBERT ARTHUR

He died in 1816 and was buried "at the mouth of the Brokenstraw under the hill." This description identifies the place as the present town of Irvineton, but the exact location of his grave has not been found.

His wife's name was Susan ——.

Robert Arthur appears as a private in the Continental Line, Northumberland County, Pa., in the list of Soldiers of the Revolution who received pay for their services, taken from a manuscript record having neither date nor title but under "Rangers on the Frontiers, 1778–1783." (Pa. Archives, 5th Series, vol. 4, p. 672.)

In the first Company of Northumberland County, Pa., Ranging Companies, 1779, under Capt. John McIllhatten, Robert Arthur was listed as First Lieutenant. (Idem, 5th Series, vol. 8, p. 673.) In the list of soldiers who received depreciation pay, as per cancelled certificates on file in the Division of Public Records, Pennsylvania State Library, the name of Robert Arthur is given in the Northumberland County Militia. (Idem, 5th Series, vol. 4, p. 358.)

Robert Arthur settled in Warren in 1798, having come down

RICHARD ARTERS

JOSIAH CHANDLER

DAVID DALRYMPLE

ELIJAH DAVIS

the Allegheny River with his family in canoes. With him were his wife and the following children: John, William, Robert, Jun., James, Boone, Samuel, Charles, Betsey, Manley and Rebecca. None of them was living in 1887. Robert, the father, later removed from Warren to a place in Brokenstraw Township. (Warren Co. History, p. vi.) On April 1, 1812, Martin Reese sold to Robert Arthur, both of Warren County, a lot in Warren, and on the same date Martin Reese and his wife Isabella sold to Robert Arthur, a lot on Liberty Street, Warren. (Warren Co. Deed Book A, p. 198, 199.) James and Arthur Andrews of Brokenstraw deeded to Robert Arthurs of the same place on Oct. 22, 1814, 150 acres and two-thirds interest in a saw mill in Brokenstraw. (Venango Co. Deed Book A, p. 524.) On Oct. 3, 1815, Obadiah Ford of Brokenstraw sold his quarter interest in a saw mill on Brokenstraw Creek to Robert Arthurs. The last named on Sept. 10, 1816, agreed to sell to Martin Reese, Sen., of Conewango, three outlots in Warren which he had purchased from Cornplanter. (Idem B, pp. 153, 256.) On March 20, 1818, Robert Arthur of Warren County assigned to Mulford and Isaac Ross, late of Ohio, a three-quarter interest in a saw mill on the land of Paul Huffman and of which Paul Huffman was a quarter owner. (Idem, p. 479.)

Robert Arthur was taxed in Conewango Township 1806 to 1815 inclusive, excepting 1814 and in Brokenstraw Township 1806, 1815 to 1818 inclusive and again in 1821.

He was listed as a resident of Conewango Township in the Census of 1810.

JOHN ANDREWS, 1758-1843

He was born in Connecticut in 1758 and died in or near Warren about 1843 but the location of his grave has not been found. He married September 4, 1816, at Glastonbury, Conn., Sarah Brown, who died in 1841.

He was a pensioner of the Revolutionary War. The Pension Bureau records (Wid. File 5629) show that he was drafted at Glastonbury, Conn., in the spring of 1776 and served as a private under Capt. Eleizer Hubbard. He was sent to New London to guard the coast from the British. He was discharged and returned to Glastonbury in Sept., 1777. Later he was drafted for two months at Glastonbury and served as a private under Capt. Timothy Hale. At the end of two months he was discharged. In March, 1778, he enlisted under Capt. Elijah Wright for one year. He was engaged in building forts along the Hudson, and wintered at Horseneck. He was discharged in March, 1779. In Sept., 1779, he enlisted for two months under Capt. Samuel Wells in the Connecticut Militia, and served along the coast.

As early as 1798, John Andrews settled in Brokenstraw Township, Warren County. Being one of the earliest settlers in the County and a surveyor, he was called upon to fill many offices having to do with the boundaries of the newly organized County of Warren. In 1800, he was appointed one of the commissioners to establish the boundary lines of Warren County. In 1820, he and two others were appointed to "lay off this county into convenient townships." He held many county offices. He was the first commissioners' clerk, having been appointed Oct. 16, 1819, when the county was organized under its own officials, having previously been attached to Crawford and later to Venango County for administrative purposes. Other offices filled by Mr. Andrews with the date of appointment were: Justice of the Peace, 1821; Burgess of Warren Borough, 1832; County Treasurer, 1835. (Warren Co. History, pp. 126, 142, 259, 297, 298, 348, lii.)

He owned a tract of land south of Irvineton and on the west side of the Allegheny River which was warranted on Feb. 3, 1806, and surveyed April 30, 1808. (Wheelock map of Warren County.) He had a mill on this land at an early date. He appears to have become a resident of Warren about 1820. In 1822, he was a member of the First Presbyterian Church of Warren, but in 1833, he became a trustee of the Methodist Church there. (Warren Co. History, pp. 370, 377.)

He was for a time a State Commissioner, authorized to sell lots in the Borough of Warren. (Idem, p. 326.) It is said that when he arrived in Brokenstraw, on April 12, 1798, he was accompanied by his step-son, Richard Dupree. (Idem, p. lii.)

His marriage was performed at Glastonbury, Conn., and there were numerous Andrews families there. In 1758, the year in which he was born, a Charles and a Steven Andrews were heads of families there. A John Andrews, son of Ephiz and Mary (Stetson) Andrews, was born in Farmington, Conn., April

25, 1757. Nothing further is known of this son. Both Glastonbury and Farmington are in Hartford County, and there is a
possibility that this John Andrews of Farmington, Conn., is the
Warren County man.

John Andrews was taxed in Warren County in 1800 and
1801; in Brokenstraw Township 1802 to 1817 inclusive, excepting
1815, and again in 1820; in Conewango Township 1806 to 1809
inclusive and 1821 to 1832 inclusive; in Warren Borough 1833
to 1843 inclusive, excepting the year 1836.

He was listed on the Warren County Census of 1800, the 1810
Census of Brokenstraw Township and the 1820 Census of Conewango Township.

John Andrews died intestate in 1843, and on July 31, 1843,
letters of administration were granted to Lansing Wetmore.
The heirs mentioned in the probate proceedings were John Mc-
Kinney and Elizabeth McKinney, formerly Elizabeth Andrews,
Isaac Davis and Margaret Davis, formerly Margaret Andrews,
Horace Watkins and Isabella Watkins, formerly Isabella An-
drews. (Warren Co. Register's Docket 2, p. 109.)

ROBERT ANDREWS, SEN.

He died between 1825 and 1830, and was buried at Youngsville, Pa., but the cemetery in which his body rested has since
been converted to other purposes and his grave has not been
located.

He was married twice. His first wife was Anna Ross but the
name of his second wife is not known.

His name appears as a private in the muster roll of Capt.
John Marshall's Company in the Second Battalion of Riflemen
in the service of the Province of Pennsylvania, under Col. Samuel
Miles, Esq., quartered near Marcus Hook, Chester County, Pa.
He enlisted March 18, 1776, in this company which was raised in
Hanover Township, Lancaster County (now Dauphin County).
(Pa. Archives, 5th Series, vol. 2, pp. 333, 336.) He was named
in the roll of the same company for the month of July, 1776.
(Idem, pp. 342, 345.) In the roll for August and September,
1776, Robert Andrews, private, was reported missing since the
battle of Aug. 27, 1776. (Idem, pp. 333, 348, 352.)

One Robert Andrews was a member of the Fourth Battalion,

Cumberland County, Pa. Militia, commanded by Col. Samuel Culbertson, May 1, 1781. (Pa. Archives, 5th Series, vol. 6, p. 283)

Robert Andrews, Sen., settled on Brokenstraw Creek, in Pittsfield Township, Warren County, in 1795. He built the first mill on that stream. He was twice married. By his first wife he had two daughters and a son John, and by his second wife four sons: James, Arthur, Robert and Moses, born 1803 and the only one surviving in 1887; and five daughters. (Warren Co. History, pp. 572, 573, vi.)

On Jan. 3, 1815, Robert Andrews was given a power of attorney by Thomas Leiper of Philadelphia, authorizing him to sell lands, especially in Warren County. (Venango Co. Deed Book B, p. 80.) The same month a similar power of attorney was given him by John Hubly of Lancaster, authorizing him to dispose of lands in District No. 6, Warren County. (Idem, p. 81.) On April 5, 1817, Robert Andrews, of Steubenville, Ohio, deeded to Henry Dunn of Warren County, Pa., an inlot in Warren. (Idem, p. 536.) This deed seems to bear out the tradition that he removed west but later returned to Warren County.

Robert Andrews was taxed as follows: Warren County, 1800, 1801; Brokenstraw Township, 1802 to 1816 inclusive; Conewango Township, 1806 to 1811 inclusive, excepting 1810.

In the Census of 1800, he was listed as a resident of Warren County and in 1810 as living in Brokenstraw Township.

JACOB BEETMAN, 1754-1829

He was born about 1754 and a notice of his death in the "Warren Gazette" for Aug. 13, 1829, reads as follows: "Died. On the 28th ult. in Brokenstraw township, in this County, Jacob Beetum, a soldier of the Revolution War aged about 75 years."

Jacob Beetman was pensioned for his services in the Revolution. The Pension Bureau records (File S-2984) show that he served in the Pa. Continental Line. He enlisted for the War, March 17, 1777, in Capt. George Grant's Company, Col. George Nagel's Regiment, Pa. Line. In 1783, he was discharged. He served in the battles of Monmouth, Brandywine, Germantown, Short Hills and Long Island. He was wounded at the battle of King's Bridge and taken prisoner after receiving twenty-two wounds.

Jacob Beaton, private, is named on a roll of Capt. George Grant's Company of the Ninth Pa. Regiment, commanded by Col. Richard Butler, all of the soldiers mentioned having enlisted for the duration of the War. Roll dated Sept. 10, 1779. (Pa. Archives, 5th Series, vol. 3, p. 408.) Among the abstracts of pensions on file in the Division of Public Records, Pa. State Library, is the following: "Jacob Bectum was in Ninth Pa. Regt. Was on 26th August 1778 surprised by enemy near Valentine's Hill below Tuckahoe and King's Bridge and was wounded in head and hands with swords and stabbed in four places with bayonets. His skull was fractured." (Idem, 5th Series, vol. 4, p. 555.)

One Jacob Beetam is given in the roll of Capt. James Chrystie's Company in the Corps of Pa. Infantry, commanded by Major Moore, for Dec., 1783, and Jan., Feb., March and May, 1784. (Idem, 5th Series, vol. 4, pp. 790, 799, 801, 803, 806, 815.) He signed a payroll as one of the same company on March 10, 1784, for pay due him to Dec. 1, 1783. (Idem, vol. 4, p. 793.)

An entry made Feb. 1, 1820, in a "List of U. S. Pensioners residing in Warren County, Pa., 1835" (vol. 2, p. 122), is the name of Jacob Beetman, aged 71, private, served Pa. Cont'l Line, died July 28, 1829.

In 1819, Jacob Beetem was taxed in Conewango Township and in 1823 as Jacob Beetom in Deerfield Township.

On Sept. 7, 1829, letters of administration on the estate of Jacob Beetom were granted to Archibald Tanner, the bond for same being signed also by John Hackney and John Andrews. (Warren Co. Register's Docket A, p. 106.)

His name has been spelled Beetam, Beetem, Beetom, Beetum and Beetman on various county records.

SIMON BEVIER, 1756–1835

He was born at Rochester, Ulster County, N. Y., March 17 or 27, 1756, died in Deerfield Township, Warren County, Pa., March 24, 1835, but his grave has not been located.

His second wife was Elizabeth Cantine, who received a pension after his death.

The following is a copy of the pension application of Simon Bevier. (Pension Bureau, Rej. File 817.)

"I enlisted as a private under Capt. Abraham Deyo Sept.

1776. Went to Kingsbridge, volunteered for 4 mos. from Kingsbridge to Horseneck where I was in a battle with the British troops. After 2 weeks went to White Plains, was taken sick and sent home. Enlisted next as private at Rochester, N. Y., Aug. or Sept. 1777 for 3 mos. under Major Stearns, marched to Albany, N. Y. then to Van Schaick's Island in the Hudson River, was there 1 month, thence to Saratoga where I was in a battle with the British. At the end of two months was discharged in writing. Next enlisted as a private under Capt. Andrew Bevier, at Vantine Hill, Ulster Co., N. Y. in the Spring of 1779. Col. Cantine. Was one of a party of five men of the company who went to the relief of a family in the neighborhood of Rochester, whose house had been burned by the Indians, and drove them off. On the same day a part of Col. Paulding's Regiment and some militia pursued the Indians and on the next day overtook, and defeated them and rescued part of the pillaged property. We were stationed at Rochester, 9 months when I was discharged, my enlistment ending. In the Spring of 1780, I was drafted into the State troops as a private in Capt. Hardenburgh's company, Col. Paulding for 9 months. The troops were stationed at Rochester during the whole term, and I was employed as a spy, at the end of nine months was discharged. Sometime in the summer of 1781 went as a private in Capt. Peary's company and went out against the Indians and Tories, who had attacked the settlement of Warwasing about three miles from Vinay's Fort and had a battle with them, when with the assistance of a part of Col. Cantine's Regiment we forced the enemy to retreat and followed them through the woods for several days until they nearly reached the Delaware river, when we returned to Rochester. I continued to act as a spy until the end of nine months, when I was discharged. I was born in Rochester Ulster County, N. Y. March 17, 1756.''

The name of Simon Bevier was entered Aug. 14, 1833, on a "List of U. S. Pensioners, 1835–40" (vol. 2, p. 188), as a private aged 79, N. Y. Militia and a resident of Warren County.

It is said that Simon Bevier came with his family from Ulster County to what is now South West Township and there purchased 1000 acres of land from the Holland Land Company. After his death, his widow and children returned to Cayuga County, N. Y. His son Elijah was the only one of the family who remained in South West Township. (Warren Co. History, pp. 538, lxxxii.)

"The Bevier Family, a history of the descendants of Louis Bevier," by Katherine Bevier, New York, 1916, contains a reference to Simon Bevier of which the following is an abstract:

Simon[4] Bevier (Johannes,[3] Abraham,[2] Louis[1]), b. March 27, 1756; d. March 24, 1835. He m. (1st) Dec. 11, 1790, Marie Bevier, b. Oct., 16, 1768; d. 1792. He m. (2d), probably in 1795, Elizabeth Cantine, b. Feb. 2, 1774; d. May 30, 1840. He lived at Wawarsing, N. Y. during his early life. He was a signer of the Articles of Association in 1775, and took part in the Revolution, being called Capt. Simon Bevier. For his services he received Land Bounty Rights. In 1795, he was a school trustee at Fantinehill, near Wawarsing. Later he removed to Sempronius Township, Cayuga County, N. Y. The towns of Niles and Owasco have since been built where he settled. He had the following children: 1. Simon. 2. Samuel, lived in Oil Creek, b. 1796; d. 1854. 3. Magdalene. 4. Peter. 5. Elijah, b. Dec. 5, 1805; d. Oct. 30, 1884. He m. in June, 1840, Leah Bevier, and resided at Owasco, N. Y. 6. Rachel. 7. Maria. 8. Andrew. 9. Margaret. (The Bevier Family, p. 114.)

The above mentioned Oil Creek probably refers to Oil Creek in Venango County, Pa., with which Warren County was included when the 1800 Census was taken. No record of Simon Bevier in Warren County is found before 1833, when his name appears on the Tax List of Deerfield Township, and is repeated year by year up to and including 1835, in which year he died, according to the Genealogy. The next year his name does not appear in the Tax List but those of the following of the name are found: Elijah, Margaret, Rachel, Magdalene, Meriah (Maria), Andrew and Samuel. In 1837, a Peter Bevier was also taxed. The names of the Beviers named in the Tax Records after 1835 are exactly the same as the names of the children of Simon as shown in the Genealogy.

WILLIAM CARPENTER

He died about 1812 and was probably buried at Garland. His will is recorded in Venango County and was probated Aug. 8, 1812. It was dated April 27, 1812, and mentioned his sons,

George, John and William, and his daughters Betsey Carpenter, Mary Evers, Rebecca Campbell, Sarah White, Rachel Carpenter and Nancy Carpenter. Executors were George Carpenter and John Mead.

His name appears in the list of the Washington County, Pa. Rangers on the Frontiers, 1778–1783. (Pa. Archives, 3d Series, vol. 23, p. 211.)

William Carpenter settled before 1806 near the present site of Garland and was active in lumbering. He owned a mill there. In 1806, he was taxed for 100 acres of land in Brokenstraw Township. In 1808, William Carpenter, Sen., was taxed for 250 acres in the same township. (Warren Co. History, pp. 128, 135, 405, 567, 572.)

William Carpenter was taxed in Oil Creek Township, Warren County, in 1801 and in Brokenstraw Township from 1802 to 1812, inclusive. In 1807, there was a William Carpenter, Jun., taxed also.

The 1800 Census lists William Carpenter as a resident of Warren County; in 1810 he is listed as living in Brokenstraw Township.

SERGT. JOSIAH CHANDLER, 1755–1840

He was born in Connecticut Jan. 9, 1755, died Oct. 30, 1840 and was buried in the Chandlers Valley Cemetery where his tombstone bears the following inscription: "Josiah Chandler, died Oct. 30, 1840, in his 86th year."

He married Eunice Dana at Pomfret, Conn., in 1781. She was born 1757 and died 1825.

For his service in the Revolution he received a pension, the application for which reads as follows:

"This day 5th of Sept. A.D. 1832, Personally appeared in open Court of the Court of Common Pleas of Warren County, Pa. Josiah Chandler, a resident of Conewango township in said county and State, aged 78, who being duly sworn makes the following declaration: that he entered the service of the United States under the following named officers and served as herein stated. He enlisted Jan. 1776, by Joseph Sawyer, a Sergt. in the company of Stephen Brown, one Sprague as lieutenant in which he served for 9 months, Col. Durkee's Regt. Thomas Grosvenor commanded one company and Captain Waterman was also in the same Regt.

"This applicant was enlisted in Pomfret, Windham County, Conn. where he resided at that time. He first marched from Pomfret to Cambridge, Mass. and from there to New London, Conn. where he took shipping and went to New York.

"He was stationed in the city of New York a short time and was then removed to Powell's Hook, where he was stationed until the enemy took possession of New York in September or October, 1776. The whole Regiment retreated from Powell's Hook to Hackensack, where they made a short halt. He was taken sick and obtained a forlough to go home.

"After getting home was taken ill with the Small Pox, in consequence of which he was not able to return until the end of the year, for which he enlisted. The applicant further stated that he enlisted for a voyage as a Marine by Geo. Richards, Chaplain and Purser of the ship Providence. Does not recollect the exact date of his discharge it having since been destroyed by fire, but thinks it was Jan. 1779. He had the Berth of a corporal aboard that ship and served about 6 months. The ship Providence, the Ranger and the Queen of France at that time were under the command of Comodore Whipple.

"The 1st lieutenant aboard the Providence was named Rathbon. The ships first sailed for Boston and fell in with the Jamaica fleet on the Banks of Newfoundland, the fleet consisted of a large number of Merchantmen under a convoy of British Vessels. We took 10 prizes, 8 of which we succeeded in bringing to Boston.

"The applicant was discharged at the close of this voyage. This applicant enlisted for another voyage as a Mariner in 1781, and served aboard the frigate Dean, 36 Guns, under command of Samuel Nicholson. He went aboard the ship, sailed in the direction of West India Islands, fell in with and captured a British ship and brought it as a prize to Boston. On the return from this voyage it was ascertained that Cornwallis had surrendered. The Marines aboard the Dean were under Capt. P——, 1st lieut. Vernon, 2d lieut. Waterman, and this applicant held the rank of Sergeant. His discharges were lost in the fire that destroyed his house and effects about 40 years ago, on the Susquehanna River in New York State. The whole amount of his services in the land and naval forces was about 1 year 9 months.

"Applicant was born in Pomfret, New London County, Conn. 1755, Jan. 9th. The record of his age may be found on the books of the Clerk of said town.

"As before stated the Applicant resided in the town of Pomfret, at the time he was called into service and since the Revolutionary War. He resided from the year 1783 to 1811, on what is called Harper's Patent, Broome County, N. Y. to which place he removed from Pomfret and from whence he removed to Sugar Grove Township, Warren County, Penn'a 1811, where he resided until the present year, from thence removed to the township of Conewango, Warren Co., Penn'a where he has resided the last 6 months."

Affidavits were made by Asa Winter, Capt. of Militia, and Judge Josiah Hall and Judah Spencer, Coroner, Dec., 1832.

His whole term of service proved to be 23 months and a certificate of pension was issued Sept. 13, 1834. (Pension Bureau File No. S-22167.)

Josiah Chandler came to Chandlers Valley from Connecticut with his son John about 1815. He was at that time an old man. (Warren Co. History, p. 437.) On Sept. 9, 1815, he purchased 100 acres of tract 310 in District No. 6, Warren County from Jesse Murphy and his wife Catharine. (Venango Co. Deed Book C, p. 63.) In 1816, he was taxed in Conewango Township. (Warren Co. History, p. 139.) On Oct. 16, 1818, he sold his 100 acres in tract 310 to Randal Evans of Warren County. (Venango Co. Deed Book C, p. 65.) In 1833 he was assessed in Conewango Township. (Warren Co. History, p. 397.)

"The Chandler Family—Descendants of William and Annis Chandler, who settled in Roxbury, Mass., 1637," by George Chandler, Worcester, Mass., 1883, contains references of which the following is an abstract:

"Josiah Chandler [6] (Josiah,[5] Philemon,[4] Philemon,[3] William,[2] William [1]), b. Jan. 9, 1756, d. Oct. 30, 1840 at Chandlers Valley, Warren County, Pa. He and his wife are buried in the graveyard set off from his farm at Chandlers Valley. He m. 1st, April 28, 1781, Eunice Dana, b. Nov. 7, 1758; d. April 26, 1825. He and his wife removed in 1791 from Pomfret, Conn., to Windsor, Broome County, N. Y. In 1810, they settled in Conewango

Township (now Sugar Grove Township), Warren County, Pa., in the valley afterwards called for Josiah Chandler and his sons, Chandlers Valley. He took up 200 acres there. At that time there was only one small settlement in the valley. His home burned in 1814. He died in the log cabin home of his daughter, Mrs. Randall Evans, near where he had lived in the valley.

"He was on the Newfoundland Banks, codfishing, when he first heard of the breaking out of the Revolutionary War in 1775. He entered as a privateer and helped take ten prizes, three of which were retaken by the British. His share of the prize money was $1,800 old continental currency. He was a pensioner." He had seven children. 1. Charles, b. 1783. 2. Celinda. 3. John, b. 1787; m. 1810, Mabel Wasson. 4. Alva. 5. Sally. 6. George. 7. Eunice. (The Chandler Family, pp. 207–8.)

Josiah Chandler was taxed in Conewango Township 1812 to 1819 inclusive and 1833 and 1844; in Sugar Grove Township 1823 and 1835.

His name is listed on the Census of Conewango Township in 1810 and in 1840 as a Revolutionary soldier aged 85 and living in the household of Alva Evens, in Sugar Grove Township.

NOAH CHAPEL, 1757–1849

He was born in Coventry, Conn., in 1757, died March 23, 1849, and was buried on his farm in Farmington Township.

He married —— Farzey.

He served in the Revolution having enlisted for three years under Capt. William Richards, Jacob Kingsbury, Ensign. He received a pension. (Pension Bureau, File 40825.)

His home was near Lander and it is said that he was intensely patriotic. On Independence Day the Stars and Stripes were always floating over his home. He had the following sons: Levi, Andrew, Alanson and Shubel. (Warren Co. History, p. 588.) He also had daughters, Shubel, aged 14, Eliza, aged 16; Lydia, aged 11; and a daughter aged 9 living with him when he applied for a pension on Oct. 4, 1820. His wife was about 53 years of age at that time. (Pension Bureau File 40825.)

According to Coventry, Conn., records, a Noah Chappel, son of Simeon and Abigail (Sarl) Chappell of Lebanon and Coventry, Conn., was born March 6, 1760. Hartland, Conn., Church

Records give a Levi, son of Noah and Lydia Chapel baptized Oct. 16, 1774, Noah and Lydia Chapel having been admitted to the Church Oct. 2, 1774. In the Census of 1790 of Coventry, Conn., a Noah Chappel is listed with a household consisting of one male over 16 years of age, two males under 16 and two females.

Noah Chappell was taxed in Pine Grove Township from 1824 to 1826 inclusive and again in 1832 and 1841.

He was listed in the Census of 1830 and 1840 as a resident of Pine Grove and in the latter year as a Revolutionary soldier aged 83.

SAMUEL CLARK, 1754–1833

He was born in 1754 and a notice of his death in the "Voice of the People," for Dec. 25, 1833 reads as follows: "Died. In Conewango Township on Sunday the 15th, Mr. Samuel Clark. He was numbered among those who fought the battles of their country, in the War of the Revolution."

He married Apr. 10, 1797, Catherine Reese, who received a pension after his death.

According to the Pension Bureau records (Wid. File 2530), he enlisted in the fall of 1775 at Morristown, N. J., for three years under Capt. Baldwin and Col. Ogden of the Continental Line. He served three years and was discharged. He was in service at Germantown, Monmouth, Long Island, Staten Island, Short Hills, Ash Swamp and Newark Farms. He was a maker of brooms. His wife was about 40 years old, son Samuel 18 years, son Martin 14 years old, daughter Sally 12 years.

"On July 2, 1849, appeared in open Court David Clark, aged 40 yrs., son of Samuel Clark who died at the deponents house Dec. 15, 1833, that he was present at his death, that he left a widow Catherine Clark now aged 85 yrs. Who has since remained a widow. She was married to Samuel Clark, Apr. 10, 1797. The oldest died when a child. Jane R. who m. Jacob Miles aged about 50. Samuel Clark aged about 48. Martin R. aged about 46. Sally who m. Luther Howard and resided in the borough of Warren, is the youngest."

On Sept. 8, 1849, James Morrison made an affidavit "that he knew Samuel and Catherine Clark before their marriage when they lived in Lycoming Co., Penna in the eastern part of the state. Morrison came to Warren Co. in 1799 to find a place to . settle and on his return home learned that Catherine Clark whose maiden name was Reese had been m. to Samuel Clark and from that time up to the time of his death has known them.''

Their children were: 1. Catherine, b. Sept. 17, 1798. 2. Jane R., b. June 18, 1800. 3. Samuel, b. July 7, 1802. 4. Martin, b. Oct. 11, 1804. 5. David, b. Mar. 11, 1806. 6. Sally, b. Sept. 19, 1809.

He was taxed in Deerfield Township in the year 1822 but after that date the names of Samuel Clark, Jun., and Catherine Clark are taxed from year to year.

In the Census of 1820, he was listed as a resident of Brokenstraw Township.

DAVID DALRYMPLE, 1762-1840

He was born in Bennington, Vermont, March 12, 1762, died Aug. 22, 1840, and his tombstone and that of his third wife in the Pittsfield Cemetery bear the following record: ''David Dalrymple died Aug. 22, 1840, AE. 78 yrs. A Soldier of the Revolution. Jennette, his wife died Feb. 10, 1839. AE. 77 years.''

He married (1st) Mary Corning; (2d) Polly Richardson Fairbanks; (3d) Jenette Clark.

He enlisted under Lieut. William Taylor, Capt. Badlom, in the Second Mass. Regt., at Northbridge, Worcester County, Mass. He arrived at Springfield, July 6, 1780, and thence marched to Hartford and West Point where he remained four weeks, thence to New Jersey and back to West Point for the winter. He was discharged in July, 1781. He re-enlisted at Northbridge for three months, and served that period and was discharged in Nov., 1781. He was a pensioner. (Pension Bureau, Inv. File 22195.)

David Dalrymple, private, Mass. Militia, aged 71, is recorded as living in Warren County, Pa. (Pension Rolls, vol. 2, p. 188.)

''Mass. Soldiers and Sailors in the Revolution'' makes the following references to David Dalrymple:

''David Dalrymple, private, Capt. Peter Woodbury's Co., Col. Jacob Gerrish's regt. of guards; enlisted July 14, 1778; discharged Nov. 9, 1778; service 3 mo. 27 days at Cambridge; roll dated Lancaster; also Capt. David Jewett's Co., Col. Gerrish's regt. of guards; enlisted Nov. 10, 1778; discharged Dec. 12, 1778; service 1 mo. 6 days; travel included.

"David Dalrymple, descriptive list of men raised to reinforce Continental Army for the term of 6 months, agreeable to resolve of June 5, 1780, returned as received of Justin Ely, Commissioner, by Maj. Peter Harwood of the 6th Mass., regt. at Springfield, July 6, 1780, aged 17 yrs., stature 5 feet 11 in., complexion light; engaged from town of Northbridge; marched to camp, July 6, 1780, under command of Lieut. Taylor of 2d Mass.

"David Dalrymple, sergeant, Capt. Thomas Whipple's Co., entered service April 20, 1780; discharged Dec. 20, 1780; service 8 mo. 1 day, with guards at Rutland: enlistment 8 months." (Mass. Soldiers and Sailors in the Revolution, pp. 370, 371.)

David Dalrymple and his wife Jennette Clark, came from Colerain, Mass., to Sugar Grove in the spring of 1812. They had a family of eight children, five sons, Clark, David, Mark, Oliver and Chauncey and three daughters. His farm was two and a half miles southwest of Sugar Grove. In 1816, he was taxed in Brokenstraw Township. (Warren Co. History, pp. 140, 309, 424, 571, xxiii.)

He was taxed in Brokenstraw Township 1812 to 1822 inclusive and in Sugar Grove Township 1822 and 1829 to 1838 inclusive. During some of the later years he was probably living with his son Clark Dalrymple.

According to family records of Hannah Dalrymple, a granddaughter, David Dalrymple had the following children: by first wife Mary Corning: 1. Hark. 2. Mark. 3. Luke. 4. John. 5. Barbara. 6. Prudie. 7. Annie. By second wife Polly Richardson Fairbanks: 8. William. 9. Lydia. 10. Ephraim. 11. Corning. By third wife Jennette Clark: 12. Mark. 13. David. 14. Clark, m. Elizabeth Schoff. 15. Oliver. 16. Chauncey. 17. Anna. 18. Fanny. 19. Anna.

ELIJAH DAVIS, 1762–1823

He was born in Essex County, N. J., Oct. 2, 1762; died at Youngsville, Pa., June 20, 1823. His tombstone in the Youngsville Cemetery reads as follows: "In memory of Elijah Davis who died June 20, 1823, aged 66 years, 8 months and 20 days." He married at Elizabeth, N. J., in 1781, Desire Lytle or Littell who was born 1765 and died 1848. She was also buried in the Youngsville Cemetery.

Elijah Davis enlisted Jan. 1, 1776, in Col. Nagle's Ninth Regiment of Foot, Capt. Nicholas' Company. In Jan., 1777, he was reported in the hospital. (Pa. Archives, 5th Series, vol. 4, p. 91.)

His name appears on the roll of the Tradyfren Company of Chester County, Pa., for the year 1780, which included all persons between the ages of 53 and 18. (Idem, vol. 5, p. 616.) In the names and rank of the Invalid Regiment commanded by Col. Nichola as it was discharged on April, 1783, is the name of Elijah Davis. (Idem, vol. 4, p. 91.)

He and his family came from Northumberland County, Pa., about 1801–3, to Columbus, Warren County. They settled in 1809 on the site of the present town of Irvineton, where he and his sons operated a ferry. In 1815, he removed to Youngsville. He had a family of six sons and three daughters. One son, Abraham Davis, was born in New Jersey, March 22, 1782. (Warren Co. History, pp. 407, 411, xxv.) Elijah Davis was taxed for 100 acres in Brokenstraw Township in 1806 and 1808. He was also listed there in 1816. (Idem, pp. 128, 135, 140.)

He was taxed in Brokenstraw Township 1804 to 1823 inclusive, excepting 1807.

In the Census of 1810 and 1820, he was listed as a resident of Brokenstraw Township.

According to family records, Elijah Davis and his wife Desire Lyttle had the following children: 1. Abraham, b. Mar. 12, 1782. 2. Susannah, b. Mar. 1, 1784, m. Wm. Mead. 3. John, b. July 28, 1787. 4. Sarah, b. Jan. 16, 1790. 5. Isaac, b. May 5, 1792. 6. Elijah, b. Oct. 3, 1796. 7. William, b. Feb. 25, 1799. 8. Elizabeth, b. Aug. 9, 1801, m. Solon Pearce. 9. James, b. Oct. 2, 1804, m. Jane Martin.

The will of Elijah Davis was entered in the Register's Docket of Warren County on Feb. 11, 1824. Only the heading is given. (Register's Docket A, p. 7.)

ANDREW EVERS, 1754–1836

He was born in mid-ocean in 1754, died in Spring Creek, Warren County, Pa., July 29, 1836, and his grave in the Spring

Creek Cemetery is marked by a monument with the following inscription: ''Grandfather Andrew Evers, a Revolutionary soldier and his family rest here.''

He was a pensioner and the Pension Bureau records (Inv. File 22760) show that he was "drafted (the summer Lord Howe took New York) under Capt. Joseph McLean at Whitemarsh, Montgomery Co., Pa. Marched to Philadelphia under Col. Bull and was in Trenton, Princeton, Brunswick, Amboy, until his term expired. Drafted again 2 weeks later under Capt. John Richmond, went to Crooked Billet, Bucks Co., Pa., thence to Washington's army, crossing the Deleware and went to Bound Brook under Col. Weister. This and a regiment of regular troops sent on guard duty along the coast. A pilot betrayed them at Middlebush and they only were saved by dispersing, a few days later they rejoined the army. Was at Brandywine, White House, thence to Sweed's Ford on the Schuylkill crossing on a bridge of wagons. Had hard fighting at Valley Forge. Howe left his baggage and pursued the army toward Philadelphia. Washington interscepted communications, captured baggage and returned to Trap Tavern, Montgomery Co. Two or three weeks later I was discharged. Enlisted in April or May of the Spring following under Cornelius Sheriff, Quarter Master. Gen. Smallwood, duties to ride express, and drive wagons; served 1 year and transferred to Gen. Sullivan at Willimgton, Del. Marched to Easton, Penn. Was in his expedition against the Indians as Express Rider, and part of time as a common soldier, served 6 months in expedition and on return to Easton was discharged. Only pay for whole time of service, one shirt. Later was in scouting parties. Took oath of allegiance before Andrew Knox of Whippen Township.''

Andrew Evers and Elijah Jackson were the first settlers of Spring Creek Township; having arrived on Nov. 10, 1797, and built their cabin on the south of the State road on the Brokenstraw Creek. Soon after, Andrew Evers removed to the farm later owned by Clinton Horn, where he died. He used to say that he was a citizen of the world, having been born of Irish parentage in mid-ocean on a vessel bound for America.

In 1806 and 1808, he was taxed for 200 acres in Brokenstraw Township. He was assessed there in 1816. (Warren Co. History, pp. 128, 135, 140, 467.)

ANDREW EVERS

MOSES FARNSWORTH

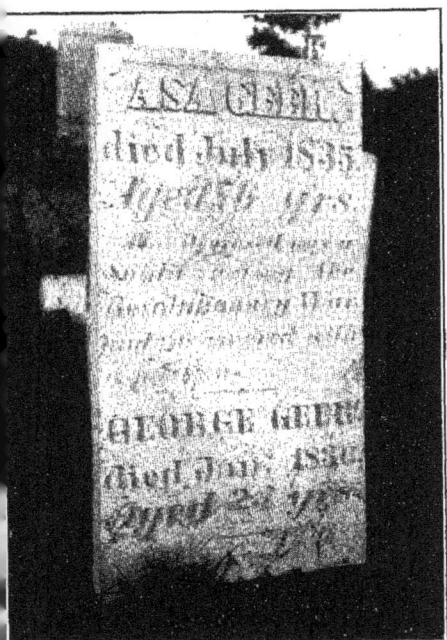

ASA GEER

HON. JOSEPH HACKNEY

He was taxed in Warren County, 1800 and 1801; in Brokenstraw Township 1802 to 1821, inclusive, and in Spring Creek Township 1822 to 1829, inclusive and again in the years 1832, 1835 and 1836.

The Census Records list Andrew Evers as follows: 1800 in Warren County; 1820 in Brokenstraw Township; and 1830 in Spring Creek Township.

On Sept. 2, 1836, letters of administration on the estate of Andrew Evers were granted to John Evers. (Warren Co. Register's Docket A, p. 262.) On Sept. 3, 1836, G. Lewis Preston and wife Sally deeded their interest in the estate of Andrew Evers to William and Francis Bates, and on Feb. 21, 1837, Nathan Taylor and wife Nancy, Francis Bates and wife Mary, William Bates and wife Tinna conveyed their interest in the estate to John Evers. (Warren Co. Deed Book G, pp. 150, 661.)

MOSES FARNSWORTH, 1753–1837

He was born Jan. 17, 1753 and died Oct. 23, 1837, at Sugar Grove. His grave in the Cherry Hill Cemetery, Sugar Grove, is marked with the following: ''Moses Farnsworth, a Revolutionary Soldier, born 1753, died 1837, aged 84 years.''

He married (1st) in Alstead, N. H., Annie Wilson and (2d) Reuhama Beckwith Crocker, b. 1765, d. 1849, aged 84 years. The dates are from her tombstone in the Cherry Hill Cemetery.

Moses Farnsworth lived at Alstead, N. H., in 1793. (New Hampshire Town Papers, vol. 2, p. 35. State Papers, vol. 14, pp. 428, 593.) He served in the Revolutionary War. (History of New Ipswich, p. 102.)

His ancestry is given in the Farnsworth Memorial, by Moses Franklin Farnsworth, 1897, p. 73, as follows: 1. Mathias of Lynn and Groton, Mass. 2. Mathias, Jun. 3. Josiah. 4. Thomas. 5. Moses.

He was taxed in Sugar Grove Township in 1825 and in Columbus Township 1827 and 1829.

SERGT. RUFUS FITCH

He was born about 1754, but the place of his birth is not known. He probably died in Chautauqua County, N. Y.

A Certificate of Pension was issued July 29, 1818, to Rufus

Fitch, care of John Groves, Esq., Auburn, Cayuga County, N. Y. The following is a copy of his application for a pension.

"On the 7th of Sept. 1820, personally appeared in the open Court of Common Pleas held in Warren County, Pa. Rufus Fitch, aged 66 years and about one month. Resident in the Township of Brokenstraw, late of M——, Cayuga Co., N. Y. who doth on his oath declare, that he served in the Revolutionary War, as follows: he enlisted as a private at Cambridge, Mass. into the Regt. of Col. Durkee, Cont'l Line, Capt. Clap's Company for 1 year from Dec. 1775, that he served faithfully until the expiration of that time. Afterward in the Spring of 1777, he enlisted for 3 years into Capt. Clap's Company, Col. Sam'l Wylly's Regt., being to the best of his recollection the 2d Regt. of the Conn. Line that he enlisted as a Sargeant and was ordered to do the duties of a quartermaster Sergt. for the regiment, that he served until his term of service expired, when he was honorably discharged at Morristown, N. J., that he applied for relief under the act of Congress 1818. That he received a certificate that is in the hands of Solomon G. Grover of Auburn, New York, his agent, to obtain the money due him. The declarent is unable to labor and is employed in teaching school when he can. Has two dependent daughters Arvilla aged 15, is a cripple, and Sophronia aged 11 yrs. is delicate and dependent upon him for support. Says he has no family residing with him excepting the two daughters."

Rufus Fitch removed to Chautauqua County, N. Y., as the following letter and affidavit will show:

"County of Chautauqua, N. Y. On the 10th day of April, 1830, before me appeared Isaac Fitch, who on his oath declares, that the said Rufus Fitch who signed the affidavit, is the same Rufus Fitch who has formerly drawn a Pension in the State of Penn'a. (Signed) Isaac Fitch. Sworn to before me Theron Bly, J. P."

The above affidavit was sent to Justice of the Peace Bly.

"Hon. Sir. With great gratitude I rec'd your instructions how to proceed in order to obtain a transfer, and having (as I suppose) complied therewith, send them back to you to accomplish the business and divert the papers to Harmony P. O., New York and oblige. Yours etc. Rufus Fitch. Harmony, Apr. 14, 1830."

His pension was transferred to New York April 24, 1830.

Further proof of his residence in Chautauqua County, N. Y., is that his name appears on a pension list of that place as Rufus Fitch, Sergeant, State of Conn., Date of Pension 1818, aged 71. (Soldiers of the American Revolution, Chautauqua Co., N. Y., p. 71.)

His wife taught the first school in Freehold Township at her house there in the summer of 1817, and the following year her husband, a Revolutionary soldier, conducted the school. (Warren Co. History, p. 529.)

He was taxed in Brokenstraw Township 1820, 1824 and 1825 and in Sugar Grove Township 1822 and 1823.

ASA GEER, 1759–1835

He was born in 1759, died July 1835 and was buried in the Scott Cemetery at Starbrick, Warren County, Pa. His tombstone is inscribed: "Asa Geer, died July 1835, ae. 76 years. The deceased was a soldier during the Revolutionary War and was honored with a pension."

A copy of his application for pension, in the Pension Bureau, Washington, D. C. (File S-41571) is as follows:

"Warren County, Penn'a, Sixth Judicial District. On the 8th day of September 1820, personally appeared before the Court of Common Pleas of said County, Asa Geer aged 60 years resident in Conewango Township, in said County, who being duly sworn, declares that he served in the Revolutionary War as follows: In Col. Huntington's regiment, Conn. Line, Capt. Richard's Company and was discharged by Gen'l Knox, having served six years, during which he was in the battles of Kingsbridge, Horseneck and several others. That he made his declaration Dec. 2, 1819, and received a certificate of Pension dated Jan. 13, 1820, No. 16306 issued at the Penna. Agency."

The last payment on his pension was made to June 26, 1835 (the date of his death) to Robinson Moore, attorney for Mary Geer, widow. He died in Conewango Township, Warren County, Pa., where he had resided. (Letter Oct. 1915 from Acting Auditor to Commissioner of Pensions.)

He was a taxable in Conewango Township, Warren County, in 1808, 1816, 1822, 1833. (Warren Co. History, pp. 133, 139, 396, 397.)

"The Geer Genealogy" by Walter Geer, New York, 1923, gives an account of Asa [5] Geer (Asa,[4] John,[3] Daniel,[2] George [1]), born in Connecticut in 1762; died Warren, Pa., June 1836; m. (1st) Olive Harris; (2d) Mary Stead. Children by first wife: 1. Asa Geer, lived near Athens, O. 2. Hosea Geer, m. (1st) Patty Prosser; (2d) Elizabeth ——. 3. John Geer, b. March 8, 1790, d. 1881; m. Charity Bucklaw. 4. Heber Geer, b. 1800, d. 1863; m. Elizabeth Maxwell. 5. Olive Geer, m. Jonathan Barlow. 6. Amy Geer, m. —— Riley. 7. Anna Geer, m. —— Trawl. 8. Elizabeth Geer, m. —— Barnhart. Children by second wife: 9. Caleb Geer, b. March 17, 1805, d. March 12, 1877; m. Elizabeth Fox. He resided on the Ohio River in West Virginia, opposite Port Homer, Ohio. 10. Benjamin Geer, b. March 15, 1806, d. May 5, 1866; m. (1st) Narcissa Stebbins; (2d) Mrs. Lucretia Green. 11. George Geer, d. about 1835. 12. Jesse Geer. 13. Mary Geer, m. Pooler. Lived in Brown (sic) Co., Pa. 14. Hannah Geer, m. —— Brown. Moved to Michigan. 15. Eliza Geer, m. Martin Clark. (Geer Genealogy, pp. 42, 43, 86, 87.)

There is no reference to the Revolutionary service of Asa [5] Geer but there is the following statement referring to Asa [4] Geer, father of Asa.[5]

"There is a tradition in the family that Asa Geer was a soldier in the Revolutionary War; was captured by the British and imprisoned on one of their ships in New York harbour; that he escaped by jumping overboard and swimming to the shore over a mile away, and that he received a pension from the government for his service."

Asa Geer was taxed in Conewango Township 1806 to 1833 inclusive, excepting the years 1817 and 1828, and in Warren Borough, 1834.

In the Census of 1810, he is listed as a resident of Conewango Township, 1820 as a resident of Brokenstraw and 1830 again in Conewango Township.

JOHN GEER

He was buried in the Kinzua Cemetery, Warren County, Pa., but there is no marker extant to indicate the location of his grave.

His name appears in the first class, Third Company under Capt. Martin Bowman in a return of the Tenth Battalion of

Militia in Lancaster County, Pa., commanded by Col. David Jenkins, as the officers and privates were classed in 1777. (Pa. Archives, 5th Series, p. 979.)

John Geer was one of the traverse jurors at the first court held in Warren County, in November, 1819. He was a taxable in Conewango Township, Warren County in 1822. (Warren Co. History, pp. 142, 396.)

While there is nothing to connect the John Geer given in the "Geer Genealogy" by Walter Geer, New York, 1923 (p. 26), with the John Geer of Warren County the reference may serve as a clue to his family history.

One John Geer was taxed in Conewango Township 1812, 1816 to 1825 inclusive and again in 1829 and 1831.

He was listed on the Census of 1810 and 1820 as a resident of Conewango Township.

JOHN GILSON, 1750–1811

He was born at Groton, Mass., June 14, 1750, died at Warren, Pa., March 12, 1811, and was buried in the old cemetery on the Daniel Jackson farm (now Wetmore Cemetery) at North Warren. He married Patience Graves in Sunderland, Mass., in 1769.

The exact service of John Gilson in the American Revolution has not been found but his daughter Betsy Gilson King and her brother John Gilson, Jr., often spoke of their father as a soldier of the Revolutionary War, and circumstancial evidence seems to prove the same.

His father John [4] Gilson served in the New Hampshire troops in the Revolution. John [5] Gilson married into a family whose every male member that was old enough, served as a soldier and in the heated state of public feeling existing at that time, he would have been listed and exiled if he had not shown himself a patriot. Therefore it was decided by competent judges to put his name upon the tablet on the Gen. Joseph Warren Monument at Warren, Pa.

The following references may serve as a clue to the exact service of John Gilson.

"John Gillson. List of 6 months' men raised agreeable to resolve of June 5, 1780, returned as received by Maj. Joseph Hosmer, superintendent of Middlesex Co., by Justin Ely, Commissioner, dated Springfield, Aug. 6, 1780: engaged from town of Pepperell.'' (Mass. Soldiers and Sailors in the Revolution, vol. 6, p. 458.)

"John Gilson, Pepperell, account of.''

"John Gilson, Pepperell, Account of in 1780, aged 18.'' "John Gilson. List of men mustered by Nathaniel Barber, muster master for Suffolk Co., dated Boston, Jan. 8, 1777. Major's Co., Maj. Steven's battalion of artillery.'' (Idem, vol. 6, p. 469.)

"John Gilson, private, time of entry, April 23, 1775, mentioned in payroll of Capt. Benjamin Mann's Company, in Col. James Reed's Regiment to the 1st of August, 1775, 8th company. A footnote states that Capt. Mann was of Mason and Lieut. Brewer of Marlborough. Men were from those towns and Temple, Wilton, etc.'' (Rolls of the Soldiers in the Revolutionary War. State of New Hampshire, vol. 1, p. 100.)

"John Gillson mentioned in Capt. Benjamin Mann's Co. List for Blankets.'' (Idem, vol. 1, p. 206.)

These latter references refer to John [4] Gilson, father of the Warren County John Gilson.

The ancestry of John [5] Gilson is given as John,[4] John,[3] John,[2] Joseph.[1] (History of Groton, pp. 402, 403.) Through the marriage of John [3] Gilson to Mary Shattuck, this line of Gilsons are of royal descent.

John Gilson was among the first settlers in Warren, in fact the first permanent settler, bringing his family from Olean in flat boats and canoes in May, 1803. For a short time after his arrival, he lived in a storehouse located on the northwest corner of what is now Market Street and Pennsylvania Avenue West. He stayed there until he could build a log house on land which he had bought on what is now Pennsylvania Avenue West. This land was afterward owned by Hon. Rufus King who sold part of it to the Hon. Ephraim Cowan, who built a house now standing (1925) on the spot once occupied by John Gilson's log house. The property was in possession of descendants for 97 years.

In 1824, John Gilson's sons went to Olean to get finished lumber to build a larger house on the west part of the lot. This lumber was floated down the river in raft form. From this arose the story of his family coming on a raft.

In 1806, he was taxed in Brokenstraw Township for two

inlots in Warren. He was a traverse juror in the first court of Warren County, November, 1819. (Warren Co. History, pp. 128, 142.) Among his children was John Gilson, Jun., an early settler of Barnes, Sheffield Township, Warren County. (Idem, pp. 511–523.)

John Gilson had the following children: 1. Lydia, b. Dec. 30, 1769, m. John Owens, a Revolutionary soldier. (See p. 62.) 2. Gideon, b. Dec. 1773, m. Mary Dailey. 3. Patience, b. Apr., 1775. 4. Olive, b. Nov., 1778; m. (1st) —— Cameron; (2d) —— Sands. 5. Keziah, b. 1780. 6. Samuel, b. March, 1785. 7. Pamela, b. Sept., 1787. 8. Erastus, b. April, 1789. 9. Betsey, b. Feb., 1791, m. John King. 10. Electa, b. Feb., 1794, m. —— Jackson. 11. John, Jr., b. May, 1797, m. Fidelia Ball.

John Gilson was taxed in Brokenstraw Township 1804 to 1806, inclusive, and 1812 to 1819, inclusive, excepting 1815; in Conewango Township 1806 to 1813, inclusive, excepting 1808.

In the Warren County census of 1810 he is listed as a resident of Conewango Township, in 1820 his wife is listed.

JAMES GREEN, 1761–1842

He was born 1761, died June 1, 1842, but his grave has not been located.

James Green was a pensioner of the Revolution. Records in the Pension Bureau, Washington, D. C. (Certificate 4625) show that he made a statement April 18, 1818, before Judge James W. Stevens of the Court of Common Pleas of Genesee County, N. Y., in which "deponent saith that he was in the service of his country 1778–9, State of Rhode Island, Capt. Westcott's Company, Col. Elliott's Regiment Artillery. Entire service 2 yrs. 9 months."

The following is the application of James Green for a pension, as recorded in the Pension Bureau (Inv. File 79746).

"On the 5th of Sept. 1820 personally appeared before the Court of the Commonwealth . . . James Green aged fifty-eight years and eleven mos. resident in the township of Brokenstraw in said County (Warren) late of the town of Batavia, N. Y. who being duly sworn doth on his oath declare that he enlisted about the last of March 1782 as a private into the R. I. Line of the army and into the regt. commanded by Col. Jeremiah Olney being at that time the only regt. belonging to said Line. That he first belonged to the company commanded by Capt. Wm. Allen, but was transferred to Capt. Ebenezer Macomber's Comp. That he enlisted for the term of 9 mos. and faithfully served the said term and was honorably discharged at Saratoga, N. Y. about the last of Dec. of the year aforesaid. That he was granted relief under act of 1818. Declares that he is a shoemaker by trade, but that owing to the failure of his sight, and ill health is not able to labor more than half his time, has no family residing with him excepting one daughter aged 13 yrs.''

The last payment on his pension was made Dec. 2, 1842, for the period from Mar. 4, 1842 to June 1, 1842, the date of the soldier's death, to Nathan Harned, administrator of pensioner's estate. At the date of death the soldier had been a resident of Warren Co., Pa., for the space of two years and previous thereto, he resided in Saratoga Co., N. Y. He left surviving the following children: Abigail McKee, James Greene, Christopher Greene, Nancy Olney, Alanson Greene and Polly Tuttle. (Letter from Comptroller General, March 28, 1924.)

James Green came to Brokenstraw Township in 1817, and for some time kept a shoe shop in the western part of Youngsville Borough. One James Green was a taxable in Brokenstraw Township in 1808, and again in 1816. (Warren Co. History, pp. 135, 140, 409.) In a deed of 1825, for land in Brokenstraw Township and one of 1836, for a lot in Youngsville, his name is spelled Greene. (Warren Co. Deed Book B, p. 310 and I, p. 216.)

He was taxed in Brokenstraw Township 1808, 1810, 1812, 1813, 1815, 1816, 1820 to 1826 inclusive, 1828 to 1839 inclusive and in 1841 and 1842.

In the 1800 Census he is listed as a resident of Warren County and in 1810 and 1820 as living in Brokenstraw Township. Both the Census records and tax records may refer to another James Green.

On Oct. 19, 1842, letters of administration on the estate of James Green of Brokenstraw Township were granted to his son-in-law, John McKee. His will dated March 15, 1842, probated Oct. 19, 1842, is recorded in Warren County Register's Docket 2, p. 45. It mentions the same children as given in the letter of the Comptroller General dated March 28, 1924. It also names John McKee, his son-in-law, and James Gorton McKee, probably a grandson.

HON. JOSEPH HACKNEY, 1763–1832

He was born at Little Falls, N. Y., on July 8, 1763, of Dutch parentage, and died in Warren, Pa., May 20, 1832. His monument in Oakland Cemetery, Warren, is inscribed as follows:

"In memory of Hon. Joseph Hackney who died May 20th, 1832 ae. 68 yea. 11 mos. 12 days. A soldier of the Revolution. An associate Judge of Warren County. He lived a moral life but in the 68th year of his age he renounced all dependence on his own works to trust in the merits and righteousness of Christ and died in the triumph of faith and full hope."

He married Margaret McGrady. She was born 1780, died 1854 and was buried beside her husband.

Joseph Hackney was one of the leading citizens among the pioneers of Crawford and Warren Counties. When he was seventeen he joined the Continental Army and served throughout the Revolutionary War. Later, during the years 1785–90, he served against the western Indians. In 1790, he joined a detachment of troops at Pittsburgh. They started down the Ohio River to join General Harmer at Fort Washington (now Cincinnati). At the mouth of the Muskingum, Joseph Hackney was severely wounded in the arm by a rifle ball fired by an Indian. Upon his return to Pittsburgh, he engaged in the mercantile business with Oliver Ormsby. He remained in Pittsburgh until 1794, when he removed to Meadville. In 1797, he built a frame building in Meadville and kept a store in it until 1817, when he settled in Warren. In 1800, Crawford County was organized, and four other counties, including Warren, were attached to it for administrative purposes. Joseph Hackney was one of the first county commissioners to be elected, serving during the years 1800–1802 and 1811–1814. In 1815, he and Major James Herriott, of Meadville, purchased a saw mill located on the Conewango Creek, near Irvineburg. This mill was owned and operated by Colt and Marlin as early as 1808. In 1817, Joseph Hackney became a resident of Warren. He was called Colonel, but it does not appear that he held that rank in his active military service. During 1818–19, he was a member of the State Legislature, being one of the three men elected to represent the district composed of the counties of Warren, Crawford, Erie, Mercer and Venango. In the Legislature he introduced a bill for the separate organization of Warren County. This bill was passed March 16, 1819, and provided that on and after Oct. 1, 1819, Warren County should be organized as a separate and independent County. Joseph Hackney was one of the first two Associate Judges appointed and served as such until his death. (Warren Co. History, pp. 141, 296, 332, 333.)

As early as 1808, he was the owner of six inlots in Warren. At the outbreak of the War of 1812, while a resident of Meadville, he took an active part in affairs. (Idem, pp. 133, 136.) On Sept. 3, 1816, he was given a power of attorney by Thomas Leiper, of Philadelphia, and was authorized to sell lands of said Leiper in Warren County. (Venango Co. Deed Book B, p. 240.) The same month John Hubley of Lancaster gave Joseph Hackney a similar power of attorney to sell his lands in Warren County. (Venango Co. Deed Book B, p. 239.)

Soon after 1819, he appears in a list of merchants of Warren. In 1827, he became the proprietor of the Mansion House in Warren, succeeding William Pierpoint. He was president of the Fourth of July celebration in Warren in 1829. Upon the incorporation of Warren as a borough in 1832, he was a member of the town council. In the first tax list of Warren Borough in 1833, he is called a tavern keeper. (Warren Co. History, pp. 331, 336, 337, 338, 364.)

Joseph Hackney was taxed 1806 to 1809, inclusive, and 1815 to 1832, inclusive, excepting 1825, in Conewango Township. In 1833 he was taxed in Warren Borough.

He is listed in the Census of 1820 and 1830 as a resident of Conewango Township.

His will, dated Aug. 13, 1832, probated May 23, 1833, mentions his wife Margaret, his children, Eliza Hall, Lydia Ann Hackney, Jane Hackney, Lutitia Derby and her husband Edward Derby, William Hackney, Joseph C. Hackney and Sarah Hackney. His executors were his wife Margaret, John Reynolds, John Hackney and Orris Hall. Witnesses, Timothy F. Parker and Thomas Struthers. (Warren Co. Register's Docket A, p. 131.)

His daughter Eliza married March 10, 1830, Orris Hall of Warren. She was born near Meadville, Pa., Feb. 9, 1809. (Warren Co. History, p. 650.)

BENJAMIN HUFF, 1747-1828

He was born 1747, died Nov. 10, 1828, and is buried in the old cemetery at Tidioute where his tombstone is inscribed: "Benj. Huff died Nov. 10, 1828 ae. 81 ys." His wife is buried beside him and her stone reads: "Mary wife of Benj. Huff died Jan. 10, 1830 ae. 81 ys."

His application for a pension was dated July 21, 1819, and states that he was 70 years old and "that he served as Private in the army of the U. S. in War of Rev. for 13 mos, enlisted Feb. 14, 1776 in the Co. of Capt. William C. Emby, 3d New Jersey Regt. served until March 14, 1777 having served the full term of his enlistment hon. Dis. at Morristown, Morris Co., N. J. engaged in several skirmishes and so conducted himself as to obtain the confidence of his officers and fellow soldiers." (Pension Bureau, Inv. File 39746.)

The last payment on his pension was made March 24, 1828, for the period from Sept. 4, 1827 to March 4, 1828, to Robinson Moore, attorney for the pensioner. At the date of payment the soldier had been a resident of Warren County, Pa., for twenty-five years and previous thereto had resided in Lycoming County, Pa. This payment was made on Certificate 16363, Philadelphia Agency. (Letter from Comptroller General, March 28, 1924.)

Benjamin Huff was taxed in Brokenstraw Township 1817, 1818, 1820 and 1821, in Deerfield Township 1822 to 1829 inclusive, and in Limestone Township 1830 to 1832 inclusive.

He was listed as a resident of Brokenstraw township in the Warren County Census of 1820.

ISAIAH JONES

He was born in Philadelphia about 1766 and a notice of his death in "Voice of the People," for Dec. 6, 1841, reads as follows: "Isaiah Jones, Esq., of Pine Grove tp. in this county, by some mischance fell into the Conewango Creek on the night of Wednesday the 9th ult., and was drowned. His body was found the next morning. On the evening of the 8th he was seen and spoken with by several and appeared to be very feeble. It would seem that he had left this borough (Warren) late, with the intention of going homeward. The turnpike follows for some distance along the margin of the creek—he had slipped from the road and whether from weakness or disease, cannot now be known, was unable to keep from falling into the creek. The night was dark and rainy and the road very muddy. Mr. Jones was in his 75th year. . . . He was a very early settler in our county and held the office of Justice of the Peace for many years.''

He was buried in the old cemetery near Russell or at Marshtown but the exact location of his grave is not known.

It is said that he was married twice; first to Mary Randolph and second to Mary (Polly) Lindsey, daughter of David Lindsey, a Revolutionary soldier. (See p. 42.)

He served in the Revolution as a fifer in list of Pennsylvanians in Col. Lamb's Regiment, Independent Artillery, 1777–1780. (Pa. Archives, 5th Series, vol. 3, p. 1080.) He also served eighteen months in the First Pa. Regiment, Continental Line, Fourth Company, Second Battalion under Capt. Andrew Irvine, according to a roll and muster for April, May and June, 1782, and dated July 12, 1782, which roll was furnished to the editor of the Archives by Dr. W. A. Irvine, Warren County, Pa. (Idem, 5th Series, vol. 2, p. 694.)

About 1795, Isaiah Jones left Philadelphia, and settled in the beech woods of Pine Grove and Farmington Township, Warren County. He came by the way of the Susquehanna and Sinnemahoning and thence through the wilderness of the present McKean County, to the ''Canoe Place'' on the Allegheny River. (Warren Co. History, p. 443.)

He was commissioned a Justice of the Peace July 4, 1807, and was referred to as a justice in 1816. (Warren Co. History, pp. 139, 300.)

There are many deeds of Isaiah Jones of Pine Grove on record. From 1828 to 1837, his wife is called Mary. During 1841, his wife is referred to as Polly. In 1831, he purchased a lot in Westfield, N. Y. (Chautauqua Co., N. Y., Deed Book 11, p. 363.)

He was taxed in Brokenstraw Township 1805 and 1806, in Conewango Township 1806 to 1821 inclusive and in Pine Grove Township 1822 to 1843 inclusive.

He is listed on the Census of 1810 and 1820 as a resident of Conewango Township and in 1830 as living in Pine Grove Township.

BENJAMIN HUFF

LIEUT. SOLOMON JORDAN

GEORGE LONG

JAMES MAGEE

In his will, dated Sept. 10, 1841, and probated Dec. 21, of the same year, he called himself of Pine Grove Township. He mentioned his wife Polly, and his children as follows: Marshall Jones, Rebecca Stanton, Caroline Chase, Charlotte Sturdevant, Susan Jones, Sarah Jones, Charles Jones, Jehu Jones. His executors were Asa Cook and David French. Witnesses David French and Susa French. (Warren Co. Register's Docket 2, p. 11.)

LIEUT. SOLOMON JORDAN, 1756–1846

He was born 1756, died about 1846 and was buried in the Methodist Cemetery at Garland, Pa., where his tombstone is inscribed: "Lieut. Solomon Jordan, U. S. Soldier, Rev. War."

He married Lydia ——.

For his services in the Revolution he received a pension, the application for which reads as follows:

"Dec. 20, 1820. Appeared before the Court of Common Pleas at Warren, Warren Co., Pa. Solomon Jordan of Brokenstraw Township, Warren Co. late of Lyonstown, Ontario County, New York, aged 64 yrs. last September.

"He enlisted for one year about the first of Jan. 1776, at Dorchester, Mass., in Capt. Cranston's Co. Col. Whitcomb's Regt. Mass. Line. He was in continuous service until the expiration of the year when he again enlisted into the Company of Capt. Paul Ellis of Portland, Mass. 15th Regt. commanded by Col. Timothy Bigelow of Worcester, Mass. March 24, 1777, at Portland, for the term of 3 years and continued to serve in the same until the expiration of said term of service when he was discharged at Fishkill, N. Y. He was in the battles of Saratoga and Monmouth. That he believes that April 24, 1818, he made a declaration of said services in applying for the benefit of the Act of Congress of March 18, 1818 and that the number of the Pension Certificate received was 3339. He states that by occupation a farmer and owing to a lameness in one hand is unable to perform many kinds of labor. He has no one residing with him excepting his wife Lydia, who is about 60 years old and of feeble Constitution, unable to do anything for her support."

His application was inscribed on the Rolls of New York, April 27, 1818, and a certificate of pension was issued Oct. 5,

1818, being sent to C. V. Boughton, Phelps, N. Y. The same was transferred from New York to Pennsylvania in 1821. (Pension Bureau Inv. File 39788.)

The last payment on his pension was made April 9, 1846, for the period from Sept. 4, 1845 to March 4, 1846, to E. S. Sanford, attorney for the pensioner. At date of death the soldier had been a resident of Warren County, Pa., for one year. (Letter from Comptroller General, Mar. 28, 1924.)

The following items doubtless refer to Solomon Jordan of Warren County.

"Solomon Jordan, Dorchester, private, Capt. Abraham Wheeler's Co., of Minute Men, Col. Lemuel Robinson's regt., which marched on alarm of April 19, 1775, service 9 days."

"Solomon Jordan, Gray, also given Falmouth, New Boston and Dorchester. List of men raised to serve in the Continental Army from Capt. Jonas Stevens Co., Col. Timothy Pike's (4th Cumberland Co.) regt., residence Gray (also given New Boston and Dorchester) engaged for town of Gray; joined Capt. Ellis's Co., Col. Biggelow's regt., term 3 years; reported enlisted in 1776. Also corporal Light Infantry Co., Col. Timothy Bigelow's regt., Continental Army pay accounts for service from Jan. 1, 1780. Residence Falmouth." (Mass. Soldiers and Sailors in the Revolution, vol. 8, p. 988.)

His name appears on the Tax Lists of Conewango Township 1823 to 1829 inclusive, excepting the year 1825.

In the 1840 Census of Brokenstraw Township, Warren County, he is given as a Revolutionary soldier, aged 85, living in the household of his son Elijah. This son was a soldier in the War of 1812.

DAVID LINDSEY

He died May 3, 1809, at Oil Creek, Crawford County, Pa., and was buried near the Warren County line.

Although it is not known that David Lindsey was an actual resident of Warren County, his name has been included because of the prominence of his descendants in local affairs.

On April 15, 1787, he was married at Lewistown, Mifflin County, Pa., to Sarah ——.

His widow, Sarah, aged 72, applied for a pension Oct. 2, 1843, at which date she was a resident of Cold Spring, Cattaraugus County, N. Y. (Pension Bureau R. File 6352.)

Her application states that David Lindsey enlisted in 1776, in Drury Township, Cumberland County, Pa., and served during the War as a private under Capt. Robert Burns in Pennsylvania. He was in the battles of Long Island, Brandywine and at the taking of Lord Cornwallis. That he had a scar below the knee which made him a little lame and a sword wound scar on his head. He always said that those scars were received in battle, thought to be the battle of Brandywine. After marriage, they resided at Lewistown, until 1809, when the family removed to Oil Creek, Pa., where David Lindsey soon after died. They had several children, but the only one mentioned in the application was Thomas.

Her claim for pension was rejected on account of insufficient proof of services, as required by the Act of July 7, 1835, under which she applied. This act required two witnesses who had personal knowledge of the services of the soldier and Edward Jones of Pine Grove Township, Warren County, was the only witness she could produce.

In 1854, the papers relating to the above claim were sent to David Lindsey, a son, aged 45 years, who applied to examine his mother's application. At that date she was deceased.

In an affidavit, supporting the claim of Sarah Lindsey, Edward Jones of Pine Grove Township, Warren County, Pa., stated "that he was well acquainted with David Lindsey and Sarah his wife and is well acquainted with said Sarah, that he was present when they were married at Lewistown, Mifflin County, State aforesaid, on or about April, 1787, that they were married by James Burns, a Justice of the Peace, who is now dead. That they lived as man and wife until the death of the said David Lindsey, which happened at Oil Creek in this state in 1809, that they lived happily together, that they had a number of children. . . . He doth further depose and say that he was well acquainted with said David Lindsey during the Revolutionary War. He enlisted in the winter of 1776, and served during the said war. He enlisted under the command of Capt. Robert Burns in the township of Derry, Cumberland County (now Mifflin Co.), Pa. He the said David Lindsey marched to Carlisle, thence to Ticonderoga, thence to Long Island, thence to Brandywine and was in the battle of Brandywine, thence to the state of New Jersey, thence he went to the south with General Washington and was at the capture of Cornwallis.'' This affidavit was acknowledged before Mason Fish, J. P., Sept. 30, 1843.

GEORGE LONG, 1759–1854

He was born at Martinsburg, Virginia, in 1759, died at Pittsfield, Pa., March 11, 1854, and was buried in the Long or Whitestown Cemetery near Garland and opposite the farm of J. B. Moore. His tombstone is inscribed as follows: ''George Long, a native of Virginia, Revolutionary soldier, and was at the taking of Cornwallace (sic), died at Pittsfield, Pa., March 11, 1854, in his 95th year. Depart my friends, dry up your tears, For I lie here till Christ appears.'' Near by is the gravestone of ''Isabella, wife of George Long, died Nov. 13, 1858, aged 84 years.''

He married Isabel McCormick in Aug., 1792, in Lycoming County, Pa.

As a soldier of the Revolution he received a pension. His application was dated Dec. 30, 1833, at which date he was aged 71 years. The following account of his service is taken from the Pension Bureau Records. (Wid. File 9139.) ''Volunteered the Spring of 1777, as a private under my father Col. Cookson Long. We were taken to Fort Kelly, on the Susquehanna river for defence against the Indians, remained there until the Spring of 1778, had many skirmishes in which many were killed, among them, James Culbertson, John Culbertson (father and son). That Spring we were driven from the fort by the Indians. My father then went to Virginia with his wife and family near Winchester.

''In the Spring of 1781, was sent by my father with a team of four horses to Alexandria, Virginia for a load of fish, got my load and started back, 14 miles, when a provost Guard under Genl. LaFayette, took my team and myself back to Alexandria. The wagon was loaded with ammunition and sent to Bottom Bridges (below Richmond). I then joined the army, and hauled baggage, and served with my team until the summer of 1781, was at the siege of Yorktown (as teamster). Was discharged soon after. Came to Warren 1798.''

George Long was born in Martinsburg, Virginia. In 1796 or

1798, with his wife and three children he came from the Susquehanna River and settled in the present Spring Creek Township at a place about six miles west of Garland, on the Brokenstraw Creek. Until 1801, he and his family lived with Andrew Evers, also a Revolutionary soldier (see p. 27) and then moved down the creek and built a house. In 1802, he built the first saw mill in Spring Creek on the site later occupied by the Horn mill. In 1801, he sold the land at Horn's siding to Daniel Horn. About 1811 or 1812, George Long removed to the western part of Pittsfield Township and there built another mill. In this place he spent the rest of his life. He owned 200 acres of land and was a lumberman and a farmer. In 1815 or 16, he bought the farm of William McClain. (Warren Co. History, pp. 468, 568, 569.)

Among his children were Hugh Long, born Feb. 2, 1802, the first white child born in Spring Creek Township, and a daughter Margaret Long, born at Garland, July 23, 1810. She married June 28, 1837, Samuel M. Graham of Lycoming (later Clinton County), Pa., who subsequently removed to Warren County. (Idem, pp. 685, 686, lviii.)

George Long was a taxable in Brokenstraw Township in 1806, when he owned 400 acres of land and a saw mill. He was assessed there also in 1808 and 1816. (Idem, pp. 129, 135, 140.)

The Tax Lists show that he was taxed in Warren County 1801, in Brokenstraw Township 1802 to 1847 inclusive, in Deerfield Township 1833 to 1836 inclusive and in Pittsfield Township 1848 to 1854 inclusive.

On the Census records he is listed as a resident of Warren County in 1800, of Brokenstraw Township 1810, 1820, 1830 and 1840. In the latter year he is called a Revolutionary soldier, aged 75. In the Census of 1850 of Pittsfield Township, George Long and his wife Isabell are listed as living with their son John Long, aged 56, and their ages are given as 88 and 76 respectively. He is called a farmer.

JOHN LONG, SEN.

He died in Brokenstraw Township and was probably buried in the Long Cemetery, near Garland, or at Pittsfield. It is said that he was a brother of George Long. (See p. 44.)

One John Long is mentioned in Capt. John Jack's Company,

Second Battalion, Cumberland County, Penn'a Militia, in 1778. (Pa. Archives, 5th Series, vol. 6, p. 169.)

One John Long was a private who enlisted Sept. 9, 1778, for the duration of the war, in Capt. John Alexander's Company of the Seventh Pa. Regiment commanded by Lt. Col. Samuel Hay. Dated June 16, 1779. (Idem, 5th Series, vol. 3, p. 252.)

John Long, a single man and brother of George Long lived in Spring Creek about 1806, and later in Pittsfield for a short time but did not remain long. (Warren Co. History, p. 568.)

A John Long was taxed for 200 acres in Brokenstraw Township in 1806, and for 160 acres in 1808. (Idem, pp. 129, 135.) Some John Long was a grandjuror in Warren in November, 1819. (Idem, p. 142.)

In 1815 or 1816, John and George Long bought the farm of William McClain in Pittsfield. (Idem, p. 569.) Among the original members of the Pittsfield Presbyterian Church is mentioned John Long. (Idem, p. 576.)

A man of this name once lived at Irvineton near the turn of the road leading to Tidioute. (Idem, p. 407.)

A John Long was taxed in Brokenstraw Township 1803 to 1808, inclusive. After 1808, a John Long, Jun., is taxed.

JOHN McDANIEL, 1753–1834

He was born at Oblong, N. Y., about 1753, died at Pine Grove, Warren County, Pa., Oct. 3, 1834, but the location of his grave has not been found.

He was married Jan. 1, 1794, to Bathsheba Cramplin, although according to her statement and that of her sister Jane Jewell, the date was Dec., 1782.

John McDaniel was a pensioner of the Revolution. From the Pension Bureau Records (Wid. File 18498) the following facts were obtained.

"Enlisted as a private 1775, Poughkeepsie, N. Y. under Capt. Andrew Billings, Col. James Clinton. Marched to Ticondaroga, thence to Canada, was at the capture of Fort St. John and Fort Shamble. Was taken sick, when recovered sent with others to take charge of prisoners taken at Shamble, to take them to Albany. Went to Fort George, taken sick sent to hospital, assisted in hospital until end of enlistment. Enlisted for 1 year under Col. Frederick Richmore was in New York to repel attack of the Asia, aided in building Fort Montgomery, and on Governor's Island. In battle of Long Island, company of Artillery under Capt. Carpenter who was killed at my side, ball passed through hair of head and arm was fractured. Went to Harlem Heights, soon after to New Jersey to cut dry Cedar timber to make fire rafts to float down river from Harlem. Thence with Lt. Holmes to Hackensack, Kingsbridge, White Plains, fought until detached to move two wounded officers to Peekskill. 11 months service. Drafted six times, once a Minute Man for 3 months, 2 months in Mohawk Valley, again under Major Goeve on alarm of Brant."

ARTHUR McGILL, 1764–1847

He was born 1764, died June 1, 1847, and was buried in the old cemetery at Tidioute where his tombstone and that of his wife are still standing, although the inscriptions, because of exposure to the weather, cannot be read accurately.

He was married June 15 or 19, 1798, to Elizabeth Arters who died April, 1840.

He served as a private in Cap. John Jardon's Company, Second Battalion of the Cumberland County Militia. (Pa. Archives, 5th Series, vol. 6, p. 200.)

It is said that Arthur McGill, with a blacksmith, repaired guns for Gen. Hall at Fort Meigs, near Falling Timber on Maumee River, Black Swamp.

On June 17, 1814, Arthur McGill of Venango County, Pa., deeded to Hugh Gallagher, 100 acres in District No. 7, of lands of the Holland Land Co. (Venango Co. Deed Book A, p. 466.) Arthur McGill was assessed in 1816 in Brokenstraw Township, Warren County. (Warren Co. History, p. 140.) He resided in Deerfield Township when it was organized in 1821. His oldest son James, was born 1804 and came to Deerfield with his father in 1812. (Warren Co. History, pp. 454, 460.)

The following children of Arthur McGill, Sen., were taken from a family record made by Arthur McGill, Jun., and now in the possession of B. S. Magill of Tidioute, Pa. 1. Dorcas McGill, b. Aug. 20, 1799, m. —— Hunter. 2. Mahettable, b. Nov. 8, 1801, m. —— Houser. 3. James, b. Feb. 4, 1804, m. Roda Parshall.

4. Charles, b. June 10, 1806, m. Sarah Courson. 5. Sarah, b. June 30, 1808, m. Mathew Hunter. 6. William, b. Sept. 12, 1810, m. Margaret Hartness. 7. Elizabeth, b. Nov. 4, 1812, d. May 24, 1837, m. James Green. 8. Arthur, b. July 20, 1816, m. Feb. 12, 1838, Jane Courson, b. May 25, 1821, d. Mar. 31, 1898. 9. Mary, b. Aug. 30, 1819, m. John Richardson. 10. Eliza, b. Aug. 1, 1823, d. Dec. 28, 1860, m. Hugh Miles. 11. Richard, b. Aug. 17, 1820, m. Kaziah Rebecca Mackey.

Arthur McGill was taxed in Brokenstraw Township 1812 to 1821 inclusive, in Deerfield Township 1822 to 1829 inclusive and again in 1840. From 1830 to 1849 he was taxed in Limestone Township.

He was listed as a resident of Conewango Township in the Census of 1820.

HUGH McGUIRE

He was probably born in Chester County, Pa '· ' about 1807 and was buried in or near Garland.

He married Patience — —.

As a private, he is named in a roll of Ca t . ..u Ramsay's Company, Col. Evan Evans' Regiment, Second Battalion of Chester County, Pa. Militia, dated April 24, 1778. (Pa. Archives, 5th Series, vol. 10, p. 517.)

About 1800, Hugh McGuire settled in Warren County. He had a contract with the government for carrying mail between Jamestown, Titusville and Meadville. (Warren Co. History, p. lxii.)

In 1806 he was taxed for 400 acres of land in Brokenstraw Township, Warren County. It appears that he owned lands formerly belonging to Stophel Gearhart. One of Hugh McGuire's sons was Thomas L. (Idem, pp. 129, 569, lxii.) .

Hugh McGuire was taxed in Brokenstraw Township 1805 to 1807 inclusive and after 1807, his wife Patience was listed for several years.

In the Census of 1810, Patience McGuire is listed as a resident of Brokenstraw Township. Her will, dated July 9, 1825, probated Nov., 1825, and recorded in Warren County Register's Docket A, p. 44, gives her residence as South West Township and names the following children: Michael McGuire, Mary Hilder-

GILL

SIMION MARSH

ROBERT MILES

JAMES MORRISON

brant, Margaret Crawfis, Eleanor Gilson, Thomas McGuire, Samuel McGuire, William McGuire, Matilda McGuire, Hugh McGuire, Elsie Dow, Haney Long. Her grandchildren Hugh and Patience, children of her son Samuel, were also mentioned. John Irvine and Archibald Tanner were appointed executors.

JAMES MAGEE, 1733–1823

He was born 1733, died 1823 and was buried in the old cemetery at Tidioute. His body was later removed to the new cemetery, where a family monument gives his and his wife's record as follows: "Grandparents—James Magee, Revolutionary soldier, 1733–1822. Margaret M., his wife, 1763–1844."

He married Margaret McCracken, May, 1780, in Mifflin County, Pa.

For his services in the Revolution, he received a pension, the application for which is on file in the Pension Bureau, Washington, D. C. (File Wid. 2954.)

"Personally appeared before me the subscriber James Magee of Brokenstraw Township, Warren County, Penn'a who swears that he entered the service of his country 1776, in the troop called Wilmington Greens, Captain Jonathan Rumford; from Wilmington were marched to Perth Amboy and there joined Gen. Washington and was sent over to Staten Island, and we took 8 Hessians, after that remained some time in Perth Amboy, then was marched to Trenton and crossed the Delaware there, and went to the Cross Roads above Philadelphia, by the order of Gen. Washington, raised a Liberty Pole there on account of the good news received from France that the French Court had acknowledged our independence. The time of my first enlistment being out, by the desire of Gen. Washington went with the troops up to Trenton and on Christmas we took a regiment of Hessian soldiers. When dismissed went to Wilmington and there enlisted again under Capt. Mitchell and was marched to Perth Amboy, and there was under Col. Grayson who commanded the 15th Virginia Regt. From there went to White Plains and there had skirmishes with the British, then crossed the North River to the Jerseys, was marched to Pennsylvania, and was in the battle of Brandywine and the battle of Germantown the 4th of October and not long after went into winter quarters at Valley Forge.

When the British left Phila. we pursued them and came up with them at Monmouth in the Jerseys and a number of skirmishes took place. We drove them to their shipping at Sandy Hook. Shortly after stormed the British Fort at Stony Point, under command of Gen. Wayne. Soon after took a party of British at Powell's Hook (160) without any loss. Then marched to Morristown in Jersey. For a year before this acted as Sergeant Major. From Morristown was marched to Phila. and from there towards Charlestown, S. C., under Col. Guest and fell in with the Army at Monk's Corners. Col. Washington commanded the Light Horse. Sometimes the British drove us and sometimes we drove them. The time of my enlistment being out, Col. Guest requested me to go back with some of our troops to guard Continental stores and bring said stores back to Camp, and then I got my discharge from Capt. Young, the latter end of April or first of May 1780. My discharge I sold to Robert and Thomas Duncan of Carlisle, who received all my emoluments due me except the land that they never got nor I myself ever saw my Compensation for the same.''

The above was sworn to before Isaac Connelly, J. P., in Venango County, Pa., Nov. 25, 1818. Also before Alex. McCalmont, Prothonotary of Venango County, Dec. 5, 1818.

Arthur McGill and Richard Arters made affidavits that they knew James Magee while they were serving in the Army.

On Sept. 3, 1822, James Magee, aged 87 or 88, appeared before the Court of Common Pleas of Warren County and made another application which states ''that he the said James Magee first enlisted for the term of 15 months early in the year 1776 in the state of Delaware in the Company commanded by Captain Latimore, the Regiment of Col. —— not now recollected, it was called the Wilmington Greens, at the end of which term he enlisted for the term of three years in the spring of 1777 in the state of Delaware in the Company commanded by Captain Mitchel who was of the Delaware troops and attached to the Regiment commanded by Col. Grayson in the line of the state of Virginia, in the Continental establishment, that he continued to serve in the said Corps until the 24th April 1780 when he was discharged from service in the town of Cambden in the state of South Carolina. Shortly to the expiration of his term he was attached to Captain Youngs Company from whom he received his discharge. That he was in the battles of Brandywine, Paoli, Germantown and Monmouth and a number of smaller skirmishes, not now distinctly recollected or known by name.'' (Minute Book No. 1, pp. 65, 66. Prothonotary's Office, Warren County.)

A Certificate of Pension was issued to Margaret Magee, June 11, 1839, and was recorded on Roll at Philadelphia, Pa. (Pension Bureau, Wid. File 2954.)

In 1812, James Magee and wife settled three miles below the mouth of Tidioute Creek in Limestone Township (then Deerfield). They came from the eastern part of Pennsylvania and had a family of eight sons and two daughters, among them being Samuel, Henry and Alexander. (Warren Co. History, pp. 460, 494.)

James Magee was taxed in Brokenstraw Township 1818 and 1819, in Deerfield Township 1822 to 1826 inclusive, excepting 1823 and in Limestone Township 1830 to 1838 inclusive, excepting 1833 and 1834.

His name appears on the 1820 Census as a resident of Conewango Township.

On June 2, 1823, letters of administration on the estate of James McGee were granted to Margaret McGee, Thomas Magee and John McGee. (Warren Co. Register's Docket A, p. 3.)

LIEUT. SIMEON MARSH, 1753-1825

He was born 1753, died in Kinzua, Warren County, Pa., Oct. 22, 1825, and was buried in the Kinzua Cemetery where his tombstone is inscribed: ''Simion Marsh died Oct. 22, 1825 Ag'd 72 yrs. 7 m's and 22 d's.''

His wife was Jane Cole, whom he married Sept. 10, 1782. She was buried beside her husband and her tombstone shows that she died Nov. 23, 1851, aged 94 years, and 9 days.

Simeon Marsh was a pensioner of the Revolutionary War. The following account of his service is from the records of the Pension Bureau. (R. File 6921.)

He served from May to Nov., 1776, under Capt. Abraham Chambers in New Jersey. He enlisted again Nov., 1776, to June 10, 1778, with the rank of Lieutenant, in Capt. James Broderick's (or Broadhead's) Company, Col. Spencer's Regiment of the Fourth New Jersey Line commanded by General Maxwell. He was in the battles of Flatbush, Short Hills, Monmouth and

Springfield. He was discharged in June, 1779. A note from the original files states "In the month of June 1778 the army was being reduced to a less number. The officers drew lots as to whom should be retained. Simeon Marsh drew a blank and was discharged June 7, 1779."

At the time of his enlistment he lived in Wallpack Township, Sussex County, N. J. On June 13, 1818, he applied for a pension, being then 68 years of age and a resident of Wyalusing Township, Bradford County, Pa. His claim was rejected on the ground that he did not serve in the Continental Army, as required by the act of March 18, 1818, under which he applied.

In the Tax List of Kinzua Township for 1824, he was listed with no property.

DARIUS MEAD, 1764–1813

He was born 1764, died 1813 in Brokenstraw Township and was buried on the original John Andrews farm near Garland, Pa.

He married Ann Hoffman, born 1769 and died 1827.

His name appears on a muster roll of the 3d class, Tenth Battalion, Lancaster County, Pa. Militia, on tour of duty at Northumberland. He served as a substitute for Leonard Shirtz, July 12, 1781, under Col. Hunter. (Pa. Archives, 5th Series, vol. 7, p. 1018.)

In 1799, Darius Mead with his brother Joseph, removed to Warren County with their families. Darius settled on a farm which was subsequently occupied by James Bonner. Within a year or two the Mead brothers built two saw mills and a grist mill, the latter being the first of its kind in Warren County. These mills were located on the Brokenstraw Creek. Darius Mead, Sen., the father of the Revolutionary soldier, was killed by the Indians near Franklin about 1794. (Warren Co. History, pp. 404, 412.)

Darius Mead was assessed in Brokenstraw Township in 1806 for 300 acres, one saw mill and half interest in a grist mill, and in 1808, in the same township, for 500 acres, a grist mill and saw mill. (Idem, pp. 129, 135.)

He was a Justice of the Peace.

In 1800 he was taxed as a resident of Warren County and 1802 to 1813 inclusive, as living in Brokenstraw Township.

He was listed in the 1800 Census of Warren County and in the 1810 Census of Brokenstraw Township.

According to family records, Darius Mead had the following children: 1. Elsie, b. 1788, m. Wm. Arthur. 2. Ruth, b. 1790, m. Abraham Davis. 3. John, b. 1791. 4. Phillip, b. 1795. 5. Darius, b. 1798, m. Ruth Curtis. 6. Elizabeth, b. 1801. 7. David, b. 1803. 8. Joseph, b. 1807. 9. Aphahel, b. 1809. 10. Anna, b. 1813.

JOHN MEAD, 1754–1819

He was born in 1754, died June, 1819, and was buried on an island in the Allegheny River, near Youngsville, Warren County, Pa. He married in Dec., 1782, Katherine Foster.

He served as a private in the Tenth Battalion, Lancaster County, Pa. Militia, in the 5th class, under Capt. Andrew Stuart, in 1781. (Pa. Archives, 5th Series, vol. 7, p. 1022.)

On May 16, 1818, Mathew Young deeded to John Mead, both of Warren County, 200 acres in Brokenstraw Township and a half interest in a saw mill located on the east side of Brokenstraw Creek. (Venango Co. Deed Book B, p. 547.) On Oct. 31, of the same year he purchased from John Garner and his wife Ruth, a lot in Youngsville. (Idem, C, p. 81.)

Beginning with the year 1808, the Tax Lists of Warren County record a John Mead for many years as a resident of Brokenstraw but the references cannot be identified with the Revolutionary soldier.

In the Census of 1810, he was listed as a resident of Brokenstraw Township.

He had the following children: 1. William, b. 1784, m. Susan Davis. 2. John, b. 1786, m. Mary Huffman. 3. Joseph. 4. Chamber. 5. Ashel. 6. Polly, m. John Camp.

JESSE MERRILL, 1753–1833

He was born in 1753, died at Warren, Pa., in 1833 but the location of his grave has not been found.

He married Rhoda ——, and lived in Conewango Township, Warren County.

For his services in the Revolution, he received a pension, the application for which was made in Oneida County, N. Y., and was dated May 4, 1818. It states that he "enlisted at Ashfield, Mass.; Dec. 1775, for one year, under Capt. Samuel Bartlett, Col. Wards Regt. Mass. Line, that he continued to serve in said Corps, or in the service of the United States until Dec. 1776 when he was discharged from service at Peekskill, N. Y. but received no written discharge. He was in the battle of Flat Bush, L. I. and was in New York when the city was vacated by the American Army. Was in the Battle of White Plains. Was stationed at Dorchester Point, near Boston at the commencement of his tour of duty." Affidavits were made by Luther Washburn and Abiezer Perkins that they served in the same company and regiment as Jesse Merrill.

On Dec. 4, 1820, Jesse Merrill, aged 67 years and 8 months, then a resident of Conewango Township, late of Williamstown, Orange County, N. Y., appeared before the Court of Common Pleas of Warren County and declared that he enlisted at Ashfield, Mass., Dec. 1775, as private for one year and continued in the same service until 1777, when he was honorably discharged at Peekskill. He had received a pension No. 12405. He had no family excepting his wife Rhoda, aged 59 years, and a son-in-law, A. Comstock, who was residing in the county.

His pension was transferred from New York to Pennsylvania, May 31, 1821.

He appears on a "List of U. S. Pensioners residing in Warren County, Pa.," 1835 (vol. 2, p. 122) as aged 81 and having served in the Mass. Continental Line, date of pension, July 14, 1819.

The last payment on his pension (Certificate 12405) was made April 8, 1833, for the period from Sept. 4, 1832 to March 4, 1833, to Wm. E. Garrett, attorney for the pensioner. At the date of payment, the soldier had been a resident of Chautauqua County, N. Y., for the period of five years and previous thereto had resided in Warren County, Pa., for seven years. (Letter from Comptroller General, March 28, 1924.)

ROBERT MILES, 1753–1810

He was born in Pennsylvania, in 1753, died in 1810 and was buried on his farm near Sugar Grove, now owned by G. W

Younie. A tombstone marks the graves of him and his wife and bears the following words: "Robert Miles, died 1810. Cath'n Miles, died 1832." Robert Miles married Catherine Watt.

He served in Lieut. Cornelius Atkinson's Company of Rangers on the Frontier, 1778–1783; also in Capt. McCoy's Company of Militia, 1781–1782. (Pa. Archives, 3d Series, vol. 23, pp. 338, 797.)

About 1797, Robert Miles and his family became the first permanent settlers in Sugar Grove Township, on a tract of land three miles square. They came up the Allegheny River from Pittsburgh in June, 1797, in the first keel boat to reach Warren. His house was one and a half miles east of Sugar Grove. He had a family of seven children, among them Robert Miles, Jun., born April 2, 1793; Polly who married James Gray in 1811. (Warren Co. History, pp. 421, 423, 636, 665.)

It is said that he was the principal man to cut what was afterward known as the Miles Road from what is known as Shadyside, on Chautauqua Lake to Pine Grove on the Conewango, the first road opened in Southern Chautauqua County, having been cut between the years 1802 and 1804. The termination on the lake was known as Miles Landing. The object of the road was to give settlers easy access to the lake, as all salt and other like necessities were brought from Black Rock by the way of Lake Erie, the Portage Road and Chautauqua Lake. After the completion of the road and during the winter, he made a canoe from a pine tree over 5 feet in diameter. In the Spring of 1806, it was drawn to the lake and for several years was the principal carrying craft on the lake. When he came to Warren County, he brought with him a young man who tutored the Miles children and the children of such neighbors as cared to send them.

Robert Miles was taxed in Warren County 1800 to 1801 inclusive, in Brokenstraw Township 1802 to 1806 inclusive, and in Conewango Township 1806 to 1810 inclusive. After the year 1810 his property had gone into an estate.

In the Census of 1800, he was listed as a resident of Warren County and 1810 as living in Conewango Township.

On Sept. 26, 1801, Robert Miles of Warren County and William P. McClay and Charles McClay made an agreement by which the McClays were to obtain the office rights to four tracts claimed by Miles and in return for services they were to receive certain tracts. (Crawford Co. Deed Book B, p. 320.)

In 1806, Robert Miles was assessed for 1650 acres in Brokenstraw Township, and in 1808 for 1400 acres in Conewango Township. (Warren Co. History, pp. 129, 134.)

Family records give the children of Robert Miles and his wife Catherine Watt as follows: 1. Frederick, m. Katherine Catlin. 2. Robert, b. 1795, d. 1877, m. Sally Smith. 3. David, bapt. 1797, d. 1869, m. Polly Smith. 4. Polly, m. James Gray. 5. John.

SOLOMON MILES, JUN., 1764–1862

He was born at Natic, Mass., in 1764, died at Garland, Warren County, Pa., in 1862, and was buried in the Long or Whitestown Cemetery, near Garland. He married Betsey Crane of Connecticut, whose tombstone in the Long Cemetery reads: "Betsey Crane, wife of Solomon Miles, died June 23, 1837, aged 50 y. and 7 days."

It is said that his name was originally Mills, but because he had been bound out by his father to learn a trade, he changed his name to Miles and never returned to Natic.

No record of the service of Solomon Miles has been found but "Mass. Soldiers and Sailors in the Revolution" (vol. 10, p. 804) gives the following references to Solomon Mills and may serve as a clue to his exact service.

"Solomon Mills, Natick, private, Capt. Joseph Morse's Co., Col. John Paterson's regt., muster roll dated Aug. 1, 1775, enlisted Apr. 24, 1775; service 3 mos. 14 days; also company return (probably Oct. 1775)."

"Solomon Mills, descriptive list of men raised to reinforce the Continental Army for the term of six months, agreeable to resolve of June 5, 1780, returned as received of Justin Ely, Commissioner, by Brig. Gen. John Glover, at Springfield July 16, 1780, age 16 yrs., stature 5 ft. 1 in.; complexion light; engaged from town of Needham; marched to camp July 16, 1780 under command of Capt. Zebulon King."

"Solomon Mills, private, Capt. Matthew Chamber's Co., Lieut. Col. Calvin Smith's (6th) regt; return for wages; wages allowed said Mills from Dec. 7, 1781 to Dec. 31, 1782, 12 mo. 25 days; also Capt. Mason Wottles's Co., Lieut. Col. Smith's regt., return for wages; wages allowed said Mills from Dec. 1782, reported received from 6th Co.'' (Mass Soldiers & Sailors in the Revolution, vol. 10, p. 804.)

In 1814, he settled in Warren County. He had by his wife Betsey, four children, namely: Joseph, Calvin, William and Delila, and perhaps others. (Warren Co. History, p. lxix.)

Solomon Miles was taxed in Warren County as follows: in Brokenstraw Township 1815 to 1821 inclusive and again 1843 to 1846 inclusive; in Spring Creek Township 1822 to 1850 inclusive.

He was listed in the Census of Brokenstraw Township for the years 1820 and 1830 and in 1840 as a resident of Spring Creek Township.

JAMES MORRISON, SEN., 1745-1839

He was born Jan. 4, 1745, in Bucks County, Pa., died Sept. 4, 1839, at Kinzua, Warren County, and was buried in the Kinzua Cemetery where his tombstone is inscribed: ''Sacred to the memory of James Morrison senr. who was born in Bucks Co., Pa. Jan. the 4th 1745. Died Sept the 4th 1839 aged 94 years & 8 months.'' A notice of his death in the ''Democratic Advocate'' of Sept. 9, 1839, states that he died Sep. 4, 1839, at his residence in Kinzua, being aged 94 years and 8 months and that ''he was a soldier of the Revolution and one of the first settlers of this county.''

He married (1st) Margaret Rice and (2d) Martha Griffin.

For his services in the Revolution, he received a pension. His military services recorded by the Pension Bureau (S. File 23816) were as follows: He enlisted Sept., 1775, for two months as private under Capt. John Elliott. In Oct., 1776, he enlisted for four months under Capt. James Ashey. In 1777, he again enlisted for two months under Capt. Robert Samuels, Col. Buchanan. In 1778, he enlisted for three months under Col. James Armstrong. He took part in the battles of Trenton, Princeton and Morristown. He was sent out twice from Patch Valley against the Indians. For three months in the spring of 1778, he was stationed at Fort Carmichael.

James Morrison and his family were among the first settlers of Warren. There were only three log huts in Warren when they arrived. James Morrison built a log house near the fort and lived there until about 1801, when he and his family removed to Kinzua. He was the first permanent settler in Kinzua Township, living on Morrison's Island in the Allegheny. (Warren Co. History, pp. 476, lxx.)

He had sons Abel, Elijah and William. (Idem, p. 477.) In 1806, James Morrison was taxed in Brokenstraw Township and in 1808 and 1816 in Conewango Township. (Idem, pp. 129, 134, 139.)

One James Morrison was elected County Commissioner in 1833. (Idem, p. 296.)

On May 1, 1813, James Morrison bought 10 out lots in the town of Warren from Abijah Meddock and wife. (Venango Co. Deed Book A, p. 370.) He received a patent for 92 acres in Conewango Township on March 11, 1815. (Warren Co. Deed Book Y, p. 162.) James Morrison of Warren sold 135 acres in Kinzua Township on Sept. 1, 1828, to Cornelius Mastin of Penn Yan, N. Y. (Idem, C, p. 262) and on Nov. 13, 1829, he sold 375 acres more in Kinzua to Mastin. (Idem, D, p. 19.) On Jan. 11, 1833, James Morrison bought two inlots in Warren. (Idem, E, p. 147.) An Island of 34 acres in Kinzua Township was sold by James Morrison, Jr., of Conewango Township to James Morrison, Sen., of Kinzua, on March 8, 1834. (Idem, M, p. 563.) One James Morrison and Robert Arthur, Sen., bought 100 acres in Pleasant Township from Jacob Weis. (Idem, H, p. 160.)

James Morrison, Sen., was taxed as follows: in Warren County 1800 and 1801, in Brokenstraw Township 1802 to 1806 inclusive, in Conewango Township 1806 to 1821 inclusive, and in Kinzua Township 1822 to 1839 inclusive. After 1839, his property is listed as the James Morrison estate.

In the 1800 Census, he is listed as a resident of Warren County and in 1810 and 1820 as living in Conewango Township.

"The History of the Morison or Morrison Family," by Leonard A. Morrison, Boston, 1880 (pp. 418-9) contains references to James Morrison of which the following is an abstract:

James[3] Morrison (Samuel,[2] John[1]) was born Jan. 4, 1745. He was the third son of Samuel Morrison and his wife Mercy Mayse who emigrated to America in 1740 and settled in Bucks County, Penn'a after the Revolution. Later Samuel and all of his family, several of whom were mariners, located on the west bank of the Susquehanna River, near the mouth of Pine Creek. Samuel died May 5, 1801, aged 100 years and 4 months. His wife died Oct. 30, 1798, aged 82 years. James Morrison had 8 sons and 3 daughters.

The will of James Morrison of Kinzua Township was dated Aug. 24, 1838, and probated March 12, 1840. (Warren Co. Register's Docket A, p. 351.) He mentioned his wife Martha and his oldest children Samuel, John, James, William and Ephraim and his youngest children Elijah, Levi, Abel, Lucretia, Priscilla (deceased), and Rachel. His executors were named as Abraham C. Marsh and John Hamlin, both of whom renounced their right to administer, and letters of administration were granted to Abel Morrison March 12, 1840.

ENSIGN GIDEON NORTHROP, 1753–1842

He was born Nov. 11, 1753, in Amity Parish (afterwards called Woodbridge), New Haven, Conn., died June 18, 1842, and was buried in the old cemetery about one half mile east of the Preston Farm and about two miles from Lander. His tombstone reads as follows: "Gideon Northrop died June 18, 1842, ae. 89 years." He married about 1779–80, Esther Munson.

He was a pensioner of the Revolution. His application on file in the Pension Bureau, Washington, D. C. (File 22922) is as follows:

"On the 8 of Sept. (1832) personally appeared before the Court of Common Pleas of Warren County, Pa. Gideon Northrup of Pine Grove, Warren Co., Pa. aged 78 yrs. 9 mos. who being duly sworn states that he entered the service of the U. S. the first of May 1775, by enlisting with Samuel Osborne, in the Parish of Amity (now Woodbridge), Town and County of New Haven where he resided in the state of Conn. The Captain (by brevet) being the oldest Lieut. named Steele, the 2d Lieut. Parsons, Major Thompson, for term of 8 mos. He was marched from New Haven to Norwalk, where he was stationed for a few weeks. Then back to New Haven where he was detained a few weeks. Thence to Jamaica Plains near Boston. Then at Temple's farm, and Rocksbury in the same neighborhood until Jan. 1, 1776. At Rocksbury was on guard one night and I recall distinctly that about 8 P.M. a firing was commenced upon the enemy who were in Boston, and kept up all night, so as to draw the attention of the enemy in that direction, while a party of men were building a fort on Dorchester Hill, about a mile from Rocksbury. The fort was erected on a hill, and a great number of barrels filled with sand were placed so as to roll them down upon the enemy.

"I again enlisted Jan. 1, 1776 for the term of 1 yr. at Rocksbury. Rec'd the bounty from Capt. Tuttle, other officers were 1st Lieut. Catlin, 2d Lieut. Jesse Grant, 1st Sergt. Sheals, 2d Sergt. Orton, 3d Sergt. Garnet, Col. Cha's Webb. Col. Webb's son was Adjutant. We remained until the enemy evacuated Boston in the Spring, think in May. We then went to New London, where we embarked and went by water to New York. We were there until the Declaration of Independence, and until the enemy took and entered New York in the latter part of the summer, when we were obliged to retreat. I was taken sick and removed to the Jersey side where I remained until I got well. After his recovery, joined his company, crossed the Hudson again and marched to White Plains, where an engagement took place between our army and the British. The Commander-in-chief, Gen. Washington was in that fight. There were 5 or 6 men killed and 3 or 4 wounded in Capt. Tuttle's company. We were obliged to retreat into the fort at White Plains. We remained in the fort some time. The enemy at length returned to New York and we were employed in various services along the Hudson river until my time expired Jan. 1, 1777, when the company was discharged. I was taking care of a sick man, whom the Captain had ordered me to care for and was not present with Company which is the reason I did not receive a regular discharge. Was born in Amity Parish, New Haven, Conn., Nov. 11, 1753 as affirmed by a record in the Town Clerk's office. After his return from service he lived in Amity 5 or 6 years, then moved to Washington in Woodbury County, Conn., where he lived for 7 or 8 years. Then moved to Plymouth in the same state, from thence to Oneida Co., N. Y. and from thence into Penn'a upwards of a year ago, where I now reside."

Samuel Woods of Oneida Co., N. Y., made an affidavit May 22, 1832, before the Commissioner of deeds of Oneida Co., N. Y., that he enlisted at the same time as Gideon Northrup.

One Gideon M. Northrop was taxed for 100 acres in Pine Grove Township in 1822. (Warren Co. History, p. 449.) He was probably the son of the Revolutionary soldier.

ENSIGN GIDEON NORTHROP

CAPT. STEPHEN OLNEY

JOHN OWENS

ESQUIRE PHILLIPS

A Gideon Northrop was taxed in Conewango Township 1821 to 1825 inclusive, in Sugar Grove Township in 1827, and in Pine Grove Township 1828 to 1848 inclusive.

In 1840, Gideon Northrop was probably living in the household of David Northrop, a son, as the Census for that year shows one male 80 to 90 in the family.

There are several references to Gideon Northrop in "The Northrup—Northrop Genealogy," by A. J. Northrup, but the accounts are somewhat confused.

Gideon Northrop, son of Joseph, b. in Plymouth, Conn., in 1753, d. in Pine Grove, Warren County, Pa., June 18, 1842. A soldier of the Revolution. He m. (1st) Hannah Hitchcock, who d. Sept. 20, 1824, in Camden, N. Y. From Camden he removed to Pine Grove. Children: 1. Lucy, m. in 1802, Manning Barnes. 2. Anna, m. Elisha Curtis. 3. Gideon. 4. Ebenezer. 5. Jesse. 6. Medad. 7. Rebecca. 8. Daniel. 9. Merrett. 10. Hannah, m. —— Brown and Bennett Cobb. 11. David. 12. Isaac, m. Cynthia Cook. 13. Esther, m. Woodward Perkins. (Northrup—Northrop Genealogy, Unconnected Families, p. 381.)

This reference is undoubtedly the Warren County man but errs in giving him as the son of Joseph. He was probably the son of Gideon [4] Northrup (Samuel,[3] Samuel,[2] Joseph [1]), who married Esther Munse of Derby, Conn., and among other children had Gideon, born Nov. 7, 1752. (Northrup—Northrop Genealogy, p. 26.) To bear out this assumption, Woodbridge, Conn., Church Records mention a Gideon, son of Gideon Northrup, baptized Feb. 4, 1753, at Woodbridge, Conn.

Family records in the possession of descendants, show that Gideon Northrop married (1st) Hannah Hutchins and (2d) Esther Munson and that he had the following children: Eben, Isaac, Daniel, Merritt, Gideon Munson, Jesse and David.

CAPT. STEPHEN OLNEY, 1752–1841

He was born in Rhode Island, Dec. 22, 1752, died at Warren, Pa., Dec. 12, 1841, and was buried in Oakland Cemetery where his tombstone is inscribed: "Stephen Olney, Capt. in the Revolution, died Dec. 12, 1841, ae. 88 years, 11 mos. and 19 da." He married Martha Aldrich, who with their son William is buried in the same plot.

He served as Ensign in Hitchcock's Rhode Island Regiment May 3 to Dec., 1775, was promoted to 1st Lieutenant of 11th Continental Infantry, Jan. 1 to Dec. 31, 1776. Served from Jan. 1 to Feb. 11, 1777, as 1st Lieutenant and then as Captain of the 2d Rhode Island Regiment. Was wounded at Springfield, June 23, 1780, and was retained in the Consolidated Regiment (1st Rhode Island Regiment) Jan. 1, 1781. Wounded at Yorktown, Oct. 14, 1781. He resigned May 1, 1782. (D. A. R. Record 6865.)

"The Genealogy of the Descendants of Thomas Olney," by James H. Olney (p. 41), contains the following account:

Stephen [5] Olney (Stephen,[4] John,[3] Epenetus,[2] Thomas [1]), b. Dec. 22, 1852, m. Martha Aldrich. He died Dec. 12, 1841. He lived in Smithfield and Glocester, R. I. He was a captain of the state militia for a number of years. Among his children was Stephen, b. Nov. 5, 1789, m. Nancy Green.

According to family records in possession of a descendant, Stephen Olney had the following children: 1. Mary, b. 1774. 2. Nathan, b. May 25, 1779. 3. Rufus, b. Oct. 23, 1782. 4. Deborah, b. Sept. 1, 1784, m. Daniel Sturdevant. 5. Cyrus, b. Jan. 1, 1787. 6. Stephen, b. Nov. 5, 1789, m. Nancy Green. 7. William, b. Feb. 24, 1792.

In the tax list of 1833, for Warren Borough, one Stephen Olney was assessed for 183 acres. In 1822, both Stephen Olney, Sen., and Jun. were taxed in Conewango Township. (Warren Co. History, pp. 396, 398.)

Stephen Olney was taxed in Conewango Township 1821 to 1824 inclusive and in 1836 and 1842; in Sugar Grove Township 1826 to 1832 inclusive and again in 1835.

In the Census of 1820, he was listed as a resident of Conewango Township and in 1830 as of Sugar Grove Township.

JOHN OWEN, 1735–1843

He was born at Salisbury, Conn., Apr. 16, 1735, died at Carroll, N. Y., Feb. 24, 1843, and was buried in the old Fifth Street Cemetery, Warren, Pa. His remains were later removed to Oakland Cemetery where a stone records that "John Owens, a soldier of the French and Revolutionary War, born at Salisbury, Conn., Ap'l 16, 1735, died at Carroll, N. Y., Feb. 24, 1843, aged 107 years 10 ms. and 8 ds."

He married Lydia Gilson, as his third wife, at Salisbury, Conn., in Aug., 1787. She was a daughter of John Gilson, a Revolutionary Soldier. (See p. 33.) She was born Jan. 30, 1773, at Sunderland, Conn., and died Nov. 7, 1851, aged 78 years, 9 months and 8 days and was buried beside her husband. After the death of John Owen she received a pension.

The Pension Bureau (Wid. File 10221) has the following record of his service: He enlisted in April or May, 1775, at Salisbury, Conn., under Capt. Nathaniel Buel, Col. Hinman to go to Ticonderoga, reaching there just after Col. Ethan Allen had taken it, served eight months as private. In May, 1776, was impressed and marched from Salisbury to Horseneck under Capt. Moore, served six months. During that time he was in a number of skirmishes between the soldiers and the ''Cowboys.'' In 1777, he marched on an alarm to Fairfield under Capt. Moore and served about two months. In 1777, went on another alarm, under Nathaniel Buel to Red Brook on the North River, service three or four weeks. He lived in Salisbury during the War. In 1792, moved to Hudson, N. Y., and lived there about 8 years, lived in Delaware County three or four years, thence to Warren County.

In the tax list of 1808, he was assessed in Conewango Township. (Warren Co. History, p. 134.)

Young's History of Chautauqua County, N. Y. (p. 244) gives an account of John Owen of which the following is an abstract:

He was a native of Windsor, Conn., and a soldier in the French Wars and in the war of the Revolution. He came with his family from the Susquehanna river, to Warren, Pa., about the year 1806, and up the Conewango in 1808. After several removals he settled on the east side of the Conewango adjoining the state line where he resided 25 or 30 years and kept a tavern or house of entertainment. He also kept a private ferry for those wishing to cross the Conewango previously to the building of the bridge. He is said to have been a very witty man. He was with the English army in the attack on Quebec in the old French War, and was a pensioner for service in the American army in the Revolutionary War. He died in Carroll, Feb. 6, 1843, aged 107 years, according to the records of Windsor, his native town. Ira Owen, a son of John Owen by his third wife, came with his father to Conewango and settled on the land east of his father. He was a soldier in the War of 1812. Reuben, the youngest son, lived with his father until his father's death and continued to live on the old homestead.

John Owen was taxed in Conewango Township, Warren County, Pa., 1806 to 1809 inclusive. In 1810 he is listed as gone.

He and his wife Lydia Gilson had the following children: 1. Betsey, b. March 23, 1788. 2. Elsey, b. July 8, 1790. 3. Ira, b. July 16, 1793. 4. Phebe, b. June 23, 1795. 5. Reuben, b. July 12, 1800. 6. Sally, b. Oct. 20, 1802.

THOMAS PAGE, 1751-1850

He was born 1751, died 1850 and was probably buried near Pittsfield.

In 1779, he was employed as an artificer in the laboratory under Col. Benj. Flower, Com. Gen. Military Stores Department, Continental Line. (Pa. Archives, 5th Series, vol. 3, p. 1131.)

He probably settled first near the Dalrymple farm at Chandlers Valley between the years 1806 and 1816. In the latter year he was assessed in Brokenstraw Township when he lived about three miles from Pittsfield on the Little Brokenstraw. His homestead passed to his son Richard. It is said that Daniel Horn was his brother-in-law. (Warren Co. History, pp. 140, 429, 570.)

On July 8, 1845, one Thomas T. Page was deeded 100 acres in tract 205, Brokenstraw Township by Harm Jan Huidekoper. (Warren Co. Deed Book K, p. 376.) On July 13, 1854, Thomas T. Page of Pittsfield, deeded a quarter acre in Wrightsville to Joel B. Tarbox. (Idem, O, p. 56.)

He was taxed in Brokenstraw Township 1811 to 1832 inclusive and in Deerfield Township 1833 to 1847, inclusive, excepting the years 1838 and 1840. In many cases he was listed as Thomas T. Page.

The will of Thomas T. Page, dated Oct. 1, 1849, probated Feb. 20, 1850, bequeathed his entire estate to his wife Margaret. Executors were Robert Donaldson and Daniel Horn. (Warren Co. Register's Docket 2, p. 417.)

JONATHAN PHELPS, 1764-1857

He was born in Lyme, Conn., in 1764, died Sept. 26, 1857, and was buried in the cemetery at Fredonia, N. Y.

He married at East Haddam, Conn., in 1784, Charity Beckwith.

His military services in the Revolution, for which he received a pension, are on record in the Pension Bureau (File 22122). The original papers in his application state that he "Enlisted as a waiter to French General Nilmantrie at Providence, Rhode Island, March or April 1781 till December 1781. From Providence to Philadelphia, thence to Yorktown, was sick, taken to Wilmington and put on sloop, provisioned 4 days, was there 14 days and nearly starved, from head of Elk, walked to Lyme, Conn. In 1782, substituted for Simeon Sanders, a Corporal in Capt. Morgan's Co. until Dec. Service 4 mos. Enlisted at Lyme, was in several skirmishes, went to Horseneck was in battle there. Enlisted Jan. 1783, under Capt. Comstock, at Fort Trumbull for 3 mos. as Corporal: Enlisted as Mariner on Brig Marshall under Capt. Dearfield for six months, captured a British Brig. After peace enlisted for 8 months at Lyme, under Capt. Josiah Burnham to protect the coast along the Sound."

"The Phelps Family of America," by A. T. Sevin (p. 286), gives facts which undoubtedly refer to Jonathan Phelps of Warren County. The following is an abstract:

Jonathan [8] Phelps (Samuel,[7] Charles,[6] William,[5] Samuel,[4] William,[3] William,[2] James [1]), son of Samuel Phelps and his wife Sarah Tiffany, was born at Lyme, Conn., 1760; married Charity Beckwith, about 1785. Mr. Phelps settled for a short time in Lyme, Conn., where one of his children was born. In 1797, appears to have been at Saratoga, N. Y., and probably went from there to Vermont. Children: 1. Rodney, b. Lyme, Conn., May 19, 1787, m. Olive Shattuck. 2. Asenath, b. Lyme, Conn. 3. Nathaniel B., b. probably at Saratoga, N. Y., 1788, m. Charity Shattuck. 4. Julia Ann, b. Saratoga, N. Y., July 12, 1797, m. Lyman, son of Thomas Shattuck. 5. Lyman, b. Saratoga, N. Y. 6. Celistia, b. Saratoga, N. Y.

Beckwith Notes (vol. 6, p. 26), mentions Charity, daughter of Nathaniel and Susanna Beckwith, born in East Haddam, May

25, 1766. Inasmuch as Jonathan Phelps had a son Nathaniel B.(eckwith?), this Charity is probably his wife.

The 1790 Census of Connecticut lists a Jonathan Phelps as a resident of Lebanon, with a household consisting of one male over 16 years of age (himself), three males under 16 and one female.

He was taxed in Sugar Grove and Spring Creek Townships, Warren County, Pa., in 1824 and in Sugar Grove Township 1826, 1827 and 1829 to 1839 inclusive.

He was listed on the 1830 Census of Sugar Grove Township.

ESQUIRE PHILLIPS, 1760–1848

He was born in Preston, Conn., Aug., 1760, died in Pine Grove, Warren County, Pa., March 19, 1848, and was buried in Fairbanks Cemetery, where a tombstone to him, his wife, and Darius and Albert Phillips reads in part: "Esquire Phillips, Soldier of '76, Died Mar. 1848, Aged 87 yrs. 7 ms."

He was married in Connecticut in 1779, to Ann Gates, who died 1838 aged 77 years.

His application for a pension states that on Sept. 4, 1832, being 72 years of age and a resident of Pine Grove, he appeared before the Court of Common Pleas of Warren County and declared "that he entered the Service of the United States, under the following officers and served as herein stated: in 1775, about the first of November I entered the service of the United States under the command of Capt. James Averill in the town of Preston, County of New London, State of Conn. and served in the capacity of a waiter to Captain Averill for 6 mos. Capt. Averill commanded a company of Militia of the Regiment of Col. Douglass of Plainfield, Conn. The lieutenants name was Cook, and the Ensign's Elisha Hutchins. Immediately after I entered we moved to Providence, R. I., from thence to Greenwich, from Greenwich to Obdyker Newtown, from there to South Kingston, from there to North Kingston where we were stationed until we were discharged, in the first of April 1776. That was at the time the British were in possession of Rhode Island.

"In the Spring following, I again enlisted in the same company, commanded by the same officers, as Minute Men, for the term of one year. Our company was composed of men who volunteered for the three Militia companies in the town of Preston, where I lived; Our officers also volunteered from each of the three companies.

"Soon after the company was organized we were ordered to march to Stonington Point, where we joined Col. Gallup's Regt. as Col. Douglass was made a General. We remained at Stonington Point two mos., and were frequently sent out with scouting parties. The Corps to which I belonged was called the Rangers. After two months we were ordered to march to Little White Plains on North River near New York. We arrived there after the battle that was fought there. We were sent out with a scouting party and fell in with a party of British and Tories at the Great Swamp a few miles distant. We had a skirmish with the British and made prisoners of about 70 British and Tories, and got 150 head of cattle and sheep. We marched with the prisoners to Norwich Town in Conn. Were then ordered back to Little White Plains, which was our headquarters. Was there two months. We were then ordered to march to New London, and were stationed there the remainder of the year, until we were discharged. Our entire service was exceedingly hard and severe during the whole year.

"I returned home and remained three days, then went as substitute for Elijah Phillips in the company commanded by Capt. Avery at Fort Griswold, as a private soldier. Remained in the Fort 3 mos. Col. Wm. Ledyard commanding. I was discharged after 3 mos. and went home. The day before I arrived at home my Father was drafted for a 3 mos. tour in the Militia. I told him that I would take his place which I did do and returned to Fort Griswold and served 3 mos. in the Fort, at the expiration of which time I was discharged. That day Col. Ledyard asked me to enlist as his Waiter, and told me that if I would do so he would return me as a 9 mos. man and that I should draw my pay. I did enlist and served under Col. Ledyard at Fort Griswold 6 mos. I believe that Col. Ledyard commanded in the Fort across the river at New London and I was backwards and forwards between the Forts, with Col. Ledyard frequently. While I was a waiter to Col. Ledyard he received a General's commission. He gave me a discharge and I went home. Was not (out?) again until the capture of Fort Griswold, at which time I was called out. I helped at that time to take care of the sick and wounded also to bury the dead. Besides this service I served in the Revolutionary War 2 yrs. and 6 mos.''

He also said that his discharge papers were lost and that he was born in Preston town. After the War he lived at Bennington, Vt., about 8 years, then moved to Homer, Courtland (Cortland) County, N. Y., and then to the county of Warren about 17 years previous to date of application.

In another deposition he gives his father's name as Jonathan Phillips.

A certificate of pension was issued July 15, 1833, and sent to J. Galbraith, Franklin, Pa. (Pension Bureau File S-14145.)

In the Census of 1820 Esquire Phillips was listed as a resident of Conewango Township; 1830 and 1840 in Pine Grove Township. In the latter year he was given as a Revolutionary soldier aged 82 years.

He had the following children: 1. Sarah, b. July 31, 1780. 2. Elisha, b. March 13, 1782. 3. Lorin, b. June 3, 1784. 4. Darius, b. July 7, 1786. 5. Lucy. 6. Jonathan. 7. Lydia. 8. Levi, b. June 24, 1795, m. Phebe Marsh. 9. Anna. 10. Maria, b. Oct. 3, 1800. 11. Elijah. 12. Albert.

JOHN PORTMAN, 1751-1833

He was born in 1751, died at Warren, Pa., Nov. 12, 1833. The location of his grave has not been found. A notice of his death in ''Voice of the People'' for Nov. 13, 1833, reads as follows: ''Died. In this Borough on Sunday last, Mr. John Portman, aged 82 years. He was an honest and industrious man and was much respected by all who knew him. He was one of the surviving remnant of worthies who achieved our National Independence—those who ought to receive the benevolent attentions of every individual of these independent states. . . .''

He married May 9, 1784, Catherine Gudling who received a pension after his death. She died Feb. 7, 1851.

The Pension Bureau Records (Wid. File 7350) show that on April 26, 1819, John Portman, aged 69, appeared before Samuel Roberts in the 5th Judicial District of Pennsylvania and made a declaration of his services. A certificate of pension was issued Sept. 30, 1819.

On June 5, 1821, being aged 71 years, he appeared before the

Court of Common Pleas of Warren County and made a declaration in order to obtain a pension. The application states "that he enlisted during the War in Aug. 1776 in Penna. in the Company commanded by Capt. Moses Carson, 8th Penna. Regt. of the Line on the Continental Establishment, Col. Enos McCoy, upon the death of McCoy commanded by Col. Broadhead and that he continued under the command of Capt. Carson until Carson revolted when the company was commanded by Capt. John Finley, with whom he served until the close of the War. He was not discharged as he was taken prisoner at the Battle of Brandywine and confined on James Island from which he escaped the evening the British evacuated Charlestown, and before he arrived at the Regiment it had been disbanded. That he was in the battles of Brandywine and Bound Brook and various skirmishes."

This application was granted and the widow's petition was founded upon it. Her pension was granted Sept. 7, 1853, although she had died Feb. 7, 1851.

In a "Letter from the Secretary of War Transmitting a Report of the Names, Rank and Line of Every Person Placed on the Pension List etc." Jan. 20, 1820 is the name of John Portman, private, Pa. Line.

According to affidavits made in 1851, by John Frew, Mary Martin and Blakely Burnes, the children of John Portman and his wife Catherine Gudling were as follows: Elizabeth, b. March, 1785, m. Dan'l McGinty, 1802; Rebecca, m. Wm. Carpenter 1804 or 1805; James, b. 1788 and was in the Mexican War; John, b. 1793; Sarah, m. —— Green; Jane, m. —— Sloan; Catherine, m. —— Washburn; Mary, m. Thomas Martin. In the affidavit of Blakely Burnes, John Portman's wife is given as Catherine Foster.

John Portman was an early settler in Pine Grove Township (then Brokenstraw) having taken up two 400-acre tracts there prior to 1806. That year he was assessed for 800 acres in Brokenstraw Township; in 1808 he was taxed for 100 acres in Conewango. He was assessed in Conewango again in 1822, and in Warren Borough in 1833. In 1819, he was a grand-juror at the first Court held in Warren County. (Warren Co. History, pp. 130, 134, 339, 396, 423, 587.)

On Nov. 30, 1830, as a resident of Warren, he deeded 400

acres in Conewango Township to Robert Miles. (Warren Co. Deed Book F, p. 539.)

He was taxed in Warren County 1800 and 1801, in Brokenstraw Township 1802 to 1806 inclusive, in Conewango Township 1806 to 1813 inclusive and again in 1819 and 1822 to 1832 inclusive. He was taxed in Warren Borough 1833 and 1834.

He was listed as a resident of Brokenstraw Township in the Census of 1810.

His will dated Nov. 9, 1832, probated Nov. 14, 1833, bequeathed his entire estate to Archibald Tanner including a note against his son John Portman. Archibald Tanner was named executor. (Warren Co. Register's Docket A, p. 191.)

JESSE PUTNAM, 1750-1837

He was born in New Hampshire in 1750, died in 1837 and was buried in the Thompson Hill Cemetery. He married about 1780 or 1781, Mrs. Rachel (Putnam) Carleton.

The record of his service in the Revolution, for which he was pensioned is as follows: (Pension Bureau, Inv. File 22459.)

"Volunteered as private, under Capt. Levi Spaulding 1776, joined the army at White Plains, was in the battle, myself and some others were detached to take charge of the baggage wagons, and get them out of the way. We succeeded in doing so, as the British did not pursue far. When my time expired was discharged at New Castle. In the following spring 1777 there was another call for men. I hired a substitute and gave him $16 per month out of my own pocket. Spring of 1778 joined with five others hired a substitute to serve during the War. Agreed to give him 20 yearling calves, and keep them until his return. When he returned four years after gave him the calves, have never received any compensation for my services or for what I paid the substitutes."

Among his children were Daniel and Edson Putnam who settled in Farmington Township in 1830. (Warren Co. History, p. lxxviii.)

"A History of the Putnam family in England and America," by Eben Putnam (p. 342), gives a statement which probably refers to the Warren County man. The following is an abstract: Jesse [6] Putnam (Dea. Ephraim,[5] Dea. Nathaniel,[4] Capt. Benjamin,[3] Nathaniel,[2] John [1]), son of Deacon Ephraim Putnam and his wife Sarah Cram, was born in Lyndeborough, N. H., Sept. 21, 1750; married Rachel, widow of Timothy Carlton of Wilton, N. H., and daughter of Nathaniel and Abigail Putnam of Wilton. Soon after his marriage they moved to Guilford, Vt., thence to Buffalo, N. Y. The names of children are not given.

ZACHEUS RAYMOND, 1766–1844

He was born in Norwalk, Conn., 1766, died Dec. 9, 1844, and was buried on the old Raymond farm, two miles from Columbus, Pa. He married in Nov., 1787, Sarah Sears, who received a pension. The Pension Bureau (Wid. File 3719) contains the original pension application, quoted below: "Enlisted in Militia at Horse Neck, Conn. 1780 or 1781 under Capt. Ebenezer Couch, Col. Waterbury, General Canfield's Brigade, served 3 months, was sent on scouting duty, had slight skirmish with Tories. Father resided at Danbury. Enlisted again for 3 months, stationed at Horseneck. May following was hired by Thaddeus Hoyt to drive cart, 2 yokes of oxen and horse to assist in moving baggage of French Army from White Plains to Annapolis, Md. to be conveyed by water to Yorktown, 25 teams in the company. Saw Washington and Lafayette at Kings Mountain. Was born Jan. 1766 at Norwalk, Conn. After the War lived at Fairfield, Conn. Thirty years ago (1802) moved to Dutchess County, N. Y. thence to Litchfield, Herkimer Co., N. Y. thence to Chenango Co., N. Y. Feb. or March 1826 moved to Columbus, Pa."

On June 1, 1840, he was listed on a "List of Pensioners of the Revolution" as residing in Columbus Township, being aged 78.

He was taxed in Columbus Township 1828 and 1831 to 1844 inclusive.

He had a son Sears S. Raymond who lived in Columbus, Pa. (Warren Co. History, p. lxxix.)

JOHN REESE, 1731–1819

He was born 1731, died at Pine Grove (now Russell), Pa., in 1819, but the location of his grave has not been found.

A pay roll of Capt. Daniel Reiff's Company in the Berks County Militia then in the service of the United States, under date of Feb. 6, 1778, names John Reese, private, enlisted Dec. 15, 1777. (Pa. Archives, 5th Series, vol. 5, p. 273, 275.)

On April 14, 1813, Ethen Jackson and wife Agnes of Conewango Township deeded 200 acres in Conewango to John Reese. (Venango Co. Deed Book A, p. 356.) An agreement dated May 20, 1813, between James O'Hara and John Rees, assignee of Jonathan Baldwin, states that O'Hara had bought land in Conewango on which Rees had adverse possession. O'Hara agreed to sell 150 acres to Rees and to sell him 50 acres more when the patent was issued. (Venango Co. Deed Book A, p. 383.)

The Holland Land Co. deeded John Reese of Warren County, 100 acres in tract 240, District 6, Warren County, on Jan. 26, 1819. (Warren Co. Deed Book A, p. 26.)

One John Reese was admitted to the bar in Nov., 1819, at the first term of court held in Warren County. (Warren Co. History, p. 143.)

John Reese was taxed for two inlots in Warren in the Conewango Township assessment for 1808. He was assessed in the same township in 1816. (Warren Co. History, pp. 134, 139.)

The name of John Reese appears on the Tax Lists of Conewango Township from 1808 to 1853 inclusive excepting 1825, 1834, 1849 and 1851. Inasmuch as the Revolutionary soldier died in 1819, most of these assessments probably refer to a son.

JOHN RUSSELL, 1741–1819

He was born in Killeah, Ireland, in 1741, died March 23, 1819, and was buried in the Pine Grove Cemetery at Russell, Warren County, Pa., where his tombstone contains the following: "In memory of John Russell who died March 23, 1819, ae. 78 ys." His wife Mary, born in Killeah, Ireland, 1742, died 1839 at Russell, was buried beside him.

John Russell, private, who was "living in Warren County in 1817" is thus listed in the Fifth Pa. Regiment, Continental Line, under Col. Richard Butler, Lt. Col. Francis Mentges, and Major Thomas L. Moore, under date of Jan. 17, 1781. (Pa. Archives, 5th Series, vol. 3, p. 88.)

He came to America and served in the Revolution and then returned to Ireland. On Feb. 25, 1793, he sailed from Belfast, Ireland, with his wife and family.

JOHN RUSSEL

GILES WHITE

WILLIAM WORK

MATTHEW YOUNG

About 1795, he came from Philadelphia with Robert Miles and John Frew and settled in Pine Grove Township. In 1806, he was assessed for 200 acres in Brokenstraw Township. (Warren Co. History, pp. 130, 443.)

John Russell was taxed in Warren County in 1801, in Brokenstraw Township 1802 to 1806 inclusive, and in Conewango Township 1806 to 1809 inclusive.

In the Census of 1800, he was listed as a resident of Warren County and in 1810 as living in Conewango Township.

He had the following children: 1. Robert, b. in Ireland, 1782, d. at Russell, Pa., 1847. He was the founder of the present village of Russell. 2. Thomas, d. in Jamestown, N. Y., 1865. 3. John, Jr., settled in Sugar Grove. 4. Molly, m. Edward Jones. 5. Peggy, m. Michael McKinney. 6. Milly, m. —— Thompson and removed south.

DANIEL SHIRLEY, 1761-1831

He was born in New Hampshire, probably at Chester about 1761, died about 1831, at Kinzua, Warren County, Pa., and was buried in the Kinzua Cemetery.

He was a pensioner of the Revolutionary War. In the Pension Bureau (Inv. File 40412), his record is given as follows: Enlisted at Londonderry, N. H., on or about April 15, 1777, as a private under Capt. Amos Anderson, Col. Seelye, General Poor, New Hampshire Line. He was attached to Col. Seelye's Regiment, 1st N. H. He served three years when he was honorably discharged by the same Col. Seelye (spelled Scilly in the papers). He was in several engagements with the British Northern Army, and was in the battle of Monmouth, previous to the surrender of Burgoyne.

The last payment on his pension was made Nov. 17, 1831, for the period from March 4, 1831 to Sept. 4, 1831, to J. Stone, attorney for the pensioner. At the date of payment the soldier had been a resident of Warren County, Pa., for the space of six years and previous thereto had resided in Chautauqua County, N. Y. (Letter from Comptroller General, March 28, 1924.)

It is said that he was a son of John Shirley who died in Warren in 1826.

JOHN SHIRLEY

He was born in Chester, New Hampshire, died in 1826 and was buried on the Marsh farm at Kinzua.

He married Hannah Stevens in Chester, N. H.

A report of the Adjutant General, Washington, in 1909, states that he served in Capt. Runnell's Company, Col. Thomas Trask's Regiment (Second New Hampshire Regiment). A receipt roll dated Chester, N. H., Sept. 21, 1776, shows that he enlisted to serve until Dec. 1, 1776, unless sooner discharged. His name appears on a muster roll and pay roll dated Sept. 26, 1776, of men raised in Cols. Thornton's and Webster's Regiments in the State of New Hampshire, to serve in Capt. Runnel's Company, Col. Thomas Trask's Regt. at New York.

The Warren County History states that he served in the Revolution, was a pioneer of Warren County and died in 1829. He had a family of nine children. A daughter, Hannah Shirley, married John Nesmith (p. 682). Daniel Shirley, a Revolutionary soldier (see p. 73), was a son of John Shirley.

Tradition says that John Shirley was considered a great canoeist, and was in the business of carrying freight to Kinzua and other points up the river, before roads were cut through the wilderness. He was famed as the only man on the Allegheny River that could, while paddling a loaded canoe up the river at flood, light his pipe and not lose headway.

MORRIS THOMAS

He died and was buried at Kinzua, Warren County, Pa.

He was a private in the 3d class in the list of the Goshen Company of Chester Co. Pa. Militia, under Capt. Joseph Johnson, for the latter part of the year 1780, also for 1781, and in the 3d class in Capt. Evan Anderson's Company of Chester County Militia for Westwhiteland and north part of Goshen, commencing April 22, 1782; also on Oct. 7, 1782. (Pa. Archives, 5th Series, vol. 5, pp. 611, 633, 643, 652, 654.)

He was taxed in Pine Grove Township in 1832.

JOHN WATT

He was born in Ireland 1758, died and was buried in Spring Creek, Warren County, Pa.

His military record is as follows: In Pa. Archives, 5th Series, vol. 7, p. 681, appears the following enlistment paper of Pa. Militia. "John Watt, aged nineteen years, five feet six inches high, fair hair, fair complexion, born in Ireland, do voluntarily agree to serve as a substitute in the room and stead of John Harman in the First Class of Captain Hendry Kendrick's Company, of Colonel John Boyd's Regiment of Militia in the County of Lancaster, for and in consideration of Forty pounds during the space of Two months as agreed with James Cranford, sub. lieutenant for the County of Lancaster. Witness my hand this Third day of September 1777.

"JOHN WATT."

He was a private in the 4th class in Capt. Enoch Hasting's Company, First Battalion of Lancaster County, Pa., dated Nov. 10, 1781. On May 31, 1783, he was named in a list of males between 18 and 53, residing in the district of the Eighth Company of the First Battalion of Lancaster Militia, under Capt. Wm. Brisben. (Idem, 5th Series, vol. 43, p. 70.)

John Watt and his family came from Penn's Valley, Lancaster County and settled in Spring Creek about 1800. He and his wife were natives of Ireland. A son Alexander Watt, is said to have settled in Spring Creek in 1797. (Warren Co. History, pp. 672, xlvi.)

In 1807, John Watt was mentioned as a part owner in lumber rafted down the river. (Idem, p. 304.)

On March 22, 1817, one John Watts of Steubenville, Ohio, was given a deed by the Holland Land Company for 200 acres in District No. 6, Warren County. (Venango Co. Deed Book B, p. 361.)

John Watt had four children among whom were Alexander, who settled in Spring Creek, and Mary, born 1784 in Penn's Valley, who married Elijah Jackson. (Warren Co. History, pp. 672, xlv, xlix.)

John Watt was taxed in Warren County in 1800 and 1801, in Brokenstraw Township 1802 to 1814 inclusive, excepting 1807, and in Spring Creek Township 1822 and 1823.

He was listed on the 1800 Census of Warren County and the 1810 Census of Brokenstraw Township.

GILES WHITE, 1752–1813

He was born 1752, baptized in Northfield, Mass., Feb. 26, 1758, died near Garland, Warren County, Pa., April 21, 1813, and was buried in the Long or Whitestown Cemetery where his tombstone is inscribed: "Giles White, Died April 21, 1813. In the 61 year of his age." He was a son of William and Lydia (Patterson) White. He married, probably in Hadley, Mass., about 1780, Sarah Dodd, born in 1757, died in Garland, Apr. 21, 1813. She was a daughter of Ebenezer and Sarah (White) Dodd of Guilford, Conn., and Hadley, Mass. She was buried beside her husband, both having died of a camp fever then prevalent.

"Giles White, private," is thus listed in Capt. Moses Kellogg's Company, Col. Porter's Hampshire County Regiment, marched Sept. 23, 1777 and was discharged Oct. 18, 1777, service 32 days including 6 days (114 miles) travel home company marched to reinforce the Northern Army under Maj. Gen. Gates on an alarm." (Mass. Soldiers and Sailors in the Revolution, vol. 17, p. 72.)

His name was also given as of Windham Co., Vt., in a payroll of Capt. Benja. Whitney's Company, Col. Bradley's Regiment, raised to assist the High Sheriff, dated Sept. 20, 1782. He was allowed pay for five days' service, travel thirty miles. (Vermont Revolutionary Rolls, p. 804.)

In the Census of 1790, Giles White is listed as the head of a family in Halifax, Windham County, Vt., and it would appear that some time between 1777 when he served in a Hampshire County, Mass. Regiment and 1782 when he served in a Vermont troop, that he established his home in Halifax, Vt.

By 1797, Giles White had removed to Cobleskill, Schoharie County, N. Y., and a year later was in Warren County, Pa., where he built a mill for James Andrews at Garland.

In Dec., 1806, he was recommended as a suitable person to keep a house of public entertainment, this house being the first of its kind in the western part of the county. In 1808, a road was laid out from "Giles White's to John Hinds's." (Warren County History, pp. 132, 308, 363.) He was a farmer and lived about three-quarters of a mile east of Garland. (Idem, p. 567.)

He was taxed in Brokenstraw Township 1803 to 1812 inclusive, and was listed as a resident of the same township in the Census of 1810.

Giles White was sixth in descent from John [1] White, through the following line: Nathaniel,[2] Nathaniel,[3] William,[4] William,[5] Giles.[6] John White, above mentioned, emigrated to America in 1632 and settled at Cambridge, Mass. Later he removed to Hartford, Conn., where he was one of the original proprietors. (Temple and Sheldon's "History of Northfield, Mass.," pp. 152, 153, 155, 157, 564.)

Giles White had the following children: 1. Dodd, d. Oct. 26, 1844, aged 59 years. 2. Samuel, d. Mar. 26, 1853, aged 66 years, 1 month and 17 days; m. Lois ——. 3. William, b. May 2, 1789, d. Apr. 2, 1841; m. Lucy ——. He was a soldier in the War of 1812. 4. James, d. Aug. 27, 1851, aged 61 years; m. (1st) Eunice Tuttle, (2d) Sarah Carpenter. 5. Henry.

WILLIAM WORK, 1753–1840

He was born in 1753, died at Pittsfield, Warren County, Pa., Aug. 22, 1840, and was buried in the Pittsfield Cemetery where his gravestone is inscribed. "Wm. Work, U. S. Soldier Rev. War."

His military record is as follows: He was mentioned as being a private in service July, 1777, in the Second class, Fourth Battalion under Lieut. William Graham, Cumberland Co., Pa. Militia, commanded by Col. James Wilson. Also as a private in Service July, 1778, same class and Battalion, under Capt. David Bowl. He is mentioned as a private in 5th Class, of Capt. Hodges' Company of the Sixth Battalion of Cumberland County Militia, under date of Oct. 4, 1780, and in the same class and Battalion on July 30, 1781 and Aug. 1, 1782. On March 12, 1782, he was a private in the Fourth Company, 2d class of the Seventh Battalion of Cumberland County Militia, called upon to perform a tour of duty by order of council of that date. (Pa. Archives, 5th Series, vol. 6, pp. 245, 258, 403, 419, 437, 505.)

He was not married, and during his residence in Warren County, made his home with David Dalrymple.

He was taxed in Brokenstraw Township in 1820 and 1821 and in Conewango Township in 1821. In 1822 he is listed as deceased.

MATHEW YOUNG

He was born about 1755 and died in Deerfield Township, Warren County, Pa., Aug. 4, 1825, while on a visit to Charles Smith. His body was brought to Youngsville in a canoe and buried there. (Warren Co. History, p. 403.) His tombstone in the I. O. O. F. Cemetery at Youngsville, reads: "In memory of Mathew Young who died Aug. 4, 1825 aged between 65 and 70." A copper plate attached to his stone is inscribed as follows: "In memory of Mathew Young, founder of Youngsville. 1792. Died Aug. 4, 1825, aged about 70. Remains removed from old burying ground by Council Sept. 15, 1884. This lot donated by I. O. of O. F. Cemetery."

He served as a private in Major's Company, Tenth Regiment, Pa., Continental Line, on the roll dated Oct. 1, 1778, at Fredericksburg, N. Y. He is named as a private in Major James Grier's Company, Tenth Regiment, in 1780 with date of enlistment as April 9, 1777. As Mathias Young, he is mentioned as in the same Company, in the service of the United States for June, July and Aug., 1780, with the note that he was discharged June 24, 1780. (Pa. Archives, 5th Series, vol. 3, pp. 513, 532, 553, 583.)

Mathew Young was a Scotchman who settled on the present site of Youngsville in the spring of 1796. He never married. He made his home with John McKinney most of the time and as early as 1800, it is said that he carved the name Youngsville on a long flat stone where he settled. In 1807, he built the first saw mill on what was later called the Siggins water power. (Warren Co. History, pp. 402, 403, 407, 413.) By 1809, he had cleared about five or six acres in what is now Youngsville. On April 23, 1814, Samuel Welch of Ohio deeded to Mathew Young and David Coursin, 100 acres in Brokenstraw Township. (Venango Co. Deed Book A, p. 445), and on Oct. 26, 1815, David Courson and wife Ruthy of Groveland, Ontario County, N. Y., conveyed 100 acres in Brokenstraw Township to Mathew Young. (Idem, B, p. 88.) On May 16, 1818, Mathew Young deeded three parcels of land, one of 200 acres and one-half interest in a saw mill on the east side of Brokenstraw Creek to John Mead of Warren County. (Idem, B, p. 547.) The second parcel of 94 acres on Brokenstraw Creek he deeded to John Garner also of Warren County.

(Idem, C, p. 50.)   The third parcel of 56½ acres and a half interest in a saw mill on Brokenstraw Creek was also deeded to John Garner.   (Idem, C, p. 81.)

In 1806, Mathew Young was taxed for 400 acres and one-quarter interest in a saw mill in Brokenstraw Township; also the same in 1808.   In 1816, he was assessed in Brokenstraw.   He was the second County Treasurer of Warren County, having held this office from 1821 to 1823.   (Warren Co. History, pp. 130, 136, 140, 297, 403.)

He was taxed in Warren County in 1800 and 1801, in Brokenstraw Township 1802 to 1826 inclusive, excepting the years 1815, 1817 and 1818.   In the Conewango Township assessment for 1822 and 1823 he was taxed as Treasurer.

He was listed as a resident of Warren County in the Census of 1800 and of Brokenstraw in 1810.

He died intestate, John McKinney being appointed administrator of his estate on Aug. 4, 1825.   (Warren Co. Register's Docket A, p. 36.)

APPENDIX

SOLDIERS WHOSE MILITARY RECORDS HAVE NOT BEEN PROVED

SYMONDS EPPS BARKER

He died and was buried between Dugall and Columbus.

His name is given as a member of the 2d Regiment Infantry, 3d Brigade, 6th Division, Militia of Massachusetts. Discharge dated Feb. 6, 1810.

Symonds Epps Barker was 10 years old at the time of the battle of Bunker Hill but he was with his father all through the battle, probably as a powder boy. Although not a regular soldier at the time of the Revolution, he certainly had his baptism of fire.

STEPHEN CHAPMAN, 1767–1854

He died Feb. 3, 1854, and was buried at Bear Lake, Warren County, Pa., where his tombstone is inscribed: "Stephen Chapman died Feb. 3, 1854 aged 87 years." His wife Ann was buried beside him.

One Stephen Chapman appears as Corporal in the Continental Line in the list of the Invalid Regiment of Pa., commanded by Col. Lewis Nichola, as it was discharged April, 1783. (Pa. Archives, 5th Series, vol. 4, p. 90.) This Invalid Regiment was made up of soldiers not well enough for active service, who acted as a sort of home guard. They were from different parts of the country. It is possible that the Stephen Chapman who came from Connecticut to Warren County might have been the Stephen Chapman mentioned above. His grave has been decorated for many years by G. A. R. Posts as that of a Revolutionary soldier.

One Stephen Chapman was taxed in Columbus Township in 1833 and in Freehold Township 1834 to 1850 inclusive, excepting the year 1839.

He was listed on the Census of 1840 and 1850 as a resident of Freehold Township. In the latter year he was recorded as aged 83 and born in Connecticut. His wife Ann aged 72 and born in Massachusetts.

JOHN McGUIRE

He was born in Ireland; died and was buried near Garland.

One John McGuire appears in the Londonderry Company of the Second Battalion, Chester County, Pa. Militia, Capt. John Ramsey's Company, Col. Evan Evans, dated April 24, 1778. Hugh McGuire is also listed. (Pa. Archives, 5th Series, vol. 5, p. 517.)

His grave has been decorated for many years as that of a Revolutionary soldier.

JAMES MARSHALL

He died and was buried at Wrightsville, Warren County, Pa.

One of his name appears on a roll of Rangers of the Frontier, 1778–1783, Washington County, Pa. Also in Capt. John McClelland's Co., Rangers of the Frontier and Capt. Edward Simonson's 4th Co., Flying Camp Rangers of the Frontier, 1776–1782. (Pa. Archives, 3d Series, vol. 23, pp. 199, 310, 335, 348, 404.)

He was taxed in 1852 in Spring Creek Township.

TOMBSTONE INSCRIPTIONS OF REVOLUTIONARY SOLDIERS AND THEIR WIVES BURIED IN WARREN COUNTY

"Richard Arters died (1825 Aged 87 years?)" (Old Cemetery, Tidioute.)

"Mary, wife of Richard Arters ———." (Old Cemetery, Tidioute.)

"Josiah Chandler died Oct. 30, 1840, in his 86 year." (Chandlers Valley Cemetery.)

"Eunice, wife of Josiah Chandler, died April 26, 1825, in her 68 year." (Chandlers Valley Cemetery.)

"Stephen Chapman died Feb. 3, 1854, aged 87 years." (Bear Lake Cemetery.)

"Ann, wife of Stephen Chapman, died Aug. 6, 1863, aged 85 years." (Bear Lake Cemetery.)

"David Dalrymple Died Aug. 22, 1840, AE. 78 Yrs. A Soldier of the Revolution. Jennette, His Wife, Died Feb. 10, 1839, AE. 77 Yrs." (Pittsfield Cemetery.)

"In memory of Elijah Davis who died June 20, 1823, aged 60 years, 8 months and 20 days." (I. O. O. F. Cemetery, Youngsville.)

"Desire, wife of Elijah Davis, died May 18, 1843, in the 81 year of her age." (I. O. O. F. Cemetery, Youngsville.)

"Grandfather Andrew Evers, a Revolutionary Soldier & family rest here." (Spring Creek Cemetery.)

"Moses Farnsworth, a Revolutionary Soldier, born 1753, died 1837, aged 84 yrs. Reuhama Farnsworth, born 1765, died 1849, aged 84 yrs." (Cherry Hill Cemetery, Sugar Grove.)

"Asa Geer died July 1835, Aged 76 yrs. The Deceased was a Soldier during the Revolutionary War and was honored with a pension." (Scott Cemetery, Star Brick.)

"In memory of Patience, wife of John Gilson, who died April 4, 1823, aged 70 years." (Oakland Cemetery, Warren.)

"In memory of Hone. Joseph Hackney who died may 20th 1832, AE. 68 yea. 11 mo. 12 days. A soldier of the revolution, An associate Judge of Warren County Which had been organized by his influence. He lived a moral life, but in the 68th year Of his age he renounced all dependance on his own Works to trust in the merits & rightenous of Christ And died in the triumpths of faith and full Assurance of HOPE." (Oakland Cemetery, Warren.)

"Margaret Hackney 1780–1854, wife of Joseph Hackney." (Oakland Cemetery, Warren.)

"Benj. Huff Died Nov. 10, 1828, AE. 81 y's." (Old Cemetery, Tidioute.)

"Mary, wife of Benj. Huff, died Jan. 10, 1830, AE 81 y's." (Old Cemetery, Tidioute.)

"Lieut. Solomon Jordan, U. S. Soldier, Rev. War." Methodist Cemetery, Garland.)

"George Long, A native of Virginia, revolutionary soldier, and was at the taking of Cornwallace, died at Pittsfield, Pa., March 11, 1854, in his 95th year. Depart my friends, dry up your tears, For I lie here till Christ appears." (Long Cemetery, near Garland.)

"Isabella, wife of George Long, died Nov. 13, 1858, aged 84 years." (Long Cemetery, near Garland.)

"Arthur MaGill, died June 1, 1847, aged 80 years." (Old Cemetery, Tidioute.)

"Elizabeth MaGill, wife of Arthur MaGill, died April 11, 1840." (Old Cemetery, Tidioute.)

"Grandparents—James Magee, Revolutionary soldier, 1733–1822. Margaret M., his wife, 1763–1844." (New Cemetery, Tidioute.)

"Simion Marsh, died Oct. 22, 1825, Ag'd 72 yrs. 7 m's & 22 d's." (Kinzua Cemetery.)

"Jane Marsh, died Nov. 23, 1851, Ag'd 94 yrs. & 9 d's." (Kinzua Cemetery.)

"Robt. Miles, d. 1810. Cath'n Miles, d. 1832." (G. W. Younie Farm, near Sugar Grove.)

"Betsey Crane, wife of Solomon Miles, died June 23, 1837, aged 50 y. and 17 days." (Long Cemetery, near Garland.)

"Sacred to the memory of James Morrison, senr. who was born in Bucks Co., Pa., Jan. the 4th 1745. Died Sep. the 4th, 1839, aged 94 years and 8 months." (Kinzua Cemetery.)

"Gideon Northrop, died June 18, 1842, AE 89 yrs." (State Road Cemetery, near Lander.)

"Stephen Olney, Cap. in the Revolution, died Dec. 12, 1841, AE. 88 Yrs. 11 mo. 19 ds. Martha, His Wife, died Mar. 28, 1846, AE. 93 Yrs. 2 mo. 8 ds." (Oakland Cemetery, Warren.)

"John Owens, A Soldier of the French & Revolutionary War, born at Salisbury, Conn., Ap'l 16, 1735. Died at Carroll, N. Y., Feb. 24, 1843, Aged 107 Years 10 ms. & 8 days." (Oakland Cemetery, Warren.)

"Lydia Owens, consort of John Owens, born at Suderland, Connecticut, Jan. 30, 1773. Died at Carroll, N. Y., Nov. 7, 1851, aged 78 years, 9 mos. & 8 days." (Oakland Cemetery, Warren.)

"Capt. Jonathan Phelps, Died Sept. 27, 1857 In His 94 Year. Charity His Wife . . ." (stone broken). (Old Cemetery, Fredonia, N. Y.)

"Anna Gates, Wife of Esquire Phillips, Died 1838, Aged 77 Yrs. Esquire Phillips, Soldier of '76, Died Mar. 1848, Aged 87 Yrs. 7 Ms." (Fairbanks Cemetery.)

"In memory of John Russel, who died March 23, 1819, AE. 78 ys." (Pine Grove Cemetery, Russell.)

"In memory of Mary, wife of John Russell, who died Oct. 9, 1839, ae. 97 ys." (Pine Grove Cemetery, Russell.)

"Giles White, Died April 21, 1813. In the 61 year of his age." (Long Cemetery, near Garland.)

"Sarah, wife of Giles White, died April 21, 1813. In the 56 year of her age." (Long Cemetery, near Garland.)

"Wm. Work, U. S. Soldier Rev. War." (Pittsfield Cemetery.)

"In memory of Mathew Young, who died Aug. 4, 1825, aged between 65 and 70." (I. O. O. F. Cemetery, Youngsville.)

LOCATIONS OF GRAVES OF REVOLUTIONARY SOLDIERS

BEAR LAKE CEMETERY
Stephen Chapman (Tombstone).

CHANDLERS VALLEY CEMETERY
Josiah Chandler (Tombstone).

COLUMBUS, FARM NEAR
Zacheus Raymond.

FAIRBANKS CEMETERY, FARMINGTON TOWNSHIP
Esquire Phillips (Tombstone).

FREEHOLD TOWNSHIP
James Marshall.

GARLAND, METHODIST CEMETERY
Lieut. Solomon Jordan (Tombstone).

GARLAND, IN OR NEAR
William Carpenter.
Hugh McGuire.
John McGuire.
Darius Mead.

IRVINETON, AT MOUTH OF BROKENSTRAW CREEK
Lieut. Robert Arthur.

KINZUA CEMETERY
John Geer.
Simeon Marsh (Tombstone).
James Morrison, Sr. (Tombstone).
Daniel Shirley.
John Shirley.
Morris Thomas.

LANDER FARM, NEAR
Noah Chappell.

NORTH WARREN, WETMORE CEMETERY
John Gilson.

PITTSFIELD CEMETERY
David Dalrymple (Tombstone).
William Work (Tombstone).

PITTSFIELD, NEAR
Thomas Page.

PRESTON CORNERS, FARMINGTON TOWNSHIP
Gideon Northrop (Tombstone).

RUSSELL, PINE GROVE CEMETERY
John Russell (Tombstone).

SPRING CREEK CEMETERY
Andrew Evers (Tombstone).

SPRING CREEK TOWNSHIP
John Watt.

STAR BRICK, SCOTT CEMETERY
Asa Geer (Tombstone).

SUGAR GROVE, CHERRY HILL CEMETERY
Moses Farnsworth (Tombstone).

SUGAR GROVE, G. W. YOUNIE FARM
Robert Miles (Tombstone).

THOMPSON HILL CEMETERY
Jesse Putnam.

TIDIOUTE, OLD CEMETERY
Richard Arters (Tombstone).
Benjamin Huff (Tombstone).
Arthur McGill (Tombstone).

TIDIOUTE, NEW CEMETERY
James Magee (Tombstone).

WARREN, OAKLAND CEMETERY
Joseph Hackney (Tombstone).
Capt. Stephen Olney (Tombstone).
John Owen (Tombstone).

WHITESTOWN CEMETERY, PITTSFIELD TOWNSHIP
George Long (Tombstone).
John Long (Probably).
Solomon Miles.
Giles White (Tombstone).

YOUNGSVILLE
Robert Andrews, Sr.

YOUNGSVILLE, I. O. O. F. CEMETERY
Elijah Davis (Tombstone).
Mathew Young (Tombstone).

YOUNGSVILLE, ON ISLAND IN ALLEGHENY RIVER
John Mead.

WARREN COUNTY PENSIONERS

From "Report from the Secretary of War . . . in relation to the Pension Establishment of the United States," Washington, 1835 Vol. 2, Pennslyvania Pension Roll, pp. 122, 188, Warren Co., Pa.

Name	Rank	Description of Service	When Placed on Pension Roll	Commencement of Pension	Age	Remarks
Jacob Beetman	Private	Pennsylvania Cont.	Feb. 1, 1821	June 28, 1820	71	Died July 28, 1829
Samuel Clark	do	New Jersey Cont.	Jan. 16, 1821	Dec. 4, 1820	80	
Asa Gier	do	Connecticut Cont.	Jan. 13, 1820	Dec. 2, 1819	74	
James Green	do	Rhode Island Cont.	Nov. 27, 1818	April 18, 1818	73	
James Green, 1st.	do	do	Dec. 27, 1820	do	78	
Benjamin Huff	do	New Jersey Cont.	Jan. 18, 1820	July 21, 1819	85	
Jesse Merrill	do	Mass. Cont.	July 14, 1819	May 4, 1818	81	
James McGee	do	Virginia Cont.	Oct. 9, 1822	Nov. 25, 1818	100	
Daniel Shirley	do	New Hamp. Cont.	June 15, 1819	May 30, 1818	73	Transferred from New York from Mar. 4, 1826
Simon Bevier	do	New York Militia	Aug. 14, 1833	Mar. 4, 1831	79	
Jonah Cummings	Priv. and corp.	Conn. Cont. Troops	July 31, 1833	do	80	
Josiah Chandler	Priv., serg. & corp.	do	Sept. 3, 1833	do	80	
David Dalrymple	Private	Mass. Militia	Apr. 14, 1833	Mar. 4, 1831	71	
Andrew Evers	do	Penna. Militia	Jan. 9, 1834	do	80	
George Long	do	Penna. State	Dec. 30, 1833	do	71	
John McDaniel	do	N. Y. Cont. Line	Sept. 24, 1833	do	81	
James Morrison	do	Penna. Militia	Feb. 4, 1834	do	90	No report yet received of payment made
Gideon Northrop	do	Conn. Militia	June 28, 1833	do	80	
Esquire Phillips	do	Conn. Cont. Line	July 15, 1833	do	75	
Jonathan Phelps	Private and corp.	Conn. Militia	do	do	71	
Jesse Putnam	Private	New York Militia	Mar. 21, 1834	do	84	
Zaccheus Raymond	do	Conn. Militia	July 15, 1833	do	69	

WARREN COUNTY PENSIONERS

From "A Census of Pensioners for Revolutionary or military service . . . returned by the marshals under the Act for taking the Sixth Census" [1840], Washington, 1841, p. 117.

Names of Pensioners, Warren Co., Pa.	Place	Age	Names of Heads of Families with Whom Pensioner Resided, June 1, 1840
John Andrews	Warren	68	John Andrews
Solomon Jordan	Brokenstraw	85	Elijah Jordan
George Long	do	75	George Long
Zacheus Raymond	Columbus	78	Zacheus Raymond
Basheba Beels	do	88	Ezra Beels
Josiah Chandler	Sugar Grove	85	Alva Evens
Noah Chappel	Pine Grove	83	Noah Chappel
Squire Philips	do	82	Squire Philips
Gideon Northrop	do	86	David Northrop
Mrs. Hannah Smith	Southwest	71	John R. Smith
Mrs. Margaret McGee	Limestone	76	Henry McGee

INDEX TO NAMES